Diana J Sweeney
1967

The School

Handwritten note:

Al Brackman
Silvia Volunteered here
& took me on Tour of the
School 1967 in hopes of
me Volunteering —

Also by
Henry Viscardi, Jr.

A MAN'S STATURE '52
GIVE US THE TOOLS '59
A LAUGHTER IN THE LONELY NIGHT '61
A LETTER TO JIMMY '62

Handwritten:

The Abilities Story '67
But not on our Block '72
The Phoenix Child '74

The School

Henry Viscardi, Jr.

Paul S. Eriksson, Publisher
Middleburg, Vermont

Published simultaneously in Canada by
George J. McLeod, Ltd., Toronto.
Library of Congress Catalog Card Number:
64-22735.
Typography and design by Arouni.
Manufactured in the United States of
America by the Haddon Craftsmen, Inc.

First Printing November 1964
Second Printing March 1966
Third Printing April 1971
Fourth Printing October 1978

This book is dedicated to the children of the world. I have written it for their benefit. All royalties I may receive will be contributed to the Human Resources School, Albertson, L.I., New York.

Preface

This is the story of a school they said could not be—and a group of wonderful, delightful, gay and exuberant children they said did not exist.

Children hidden away? In our modern age? Children no one dares to speak of, children who rarely go out the front door, who have few friends because the youngsters up the street simply don't play with that "crippled kid in the big grey house?"

This is a story of the homebound child, not in some medieval time but today—the child for whom there is no school, no normal relationship with other youngsters, with the world outside his own home, often his own upstairs room. It is the story of children who until now have often been prisoners in a special kind of solitary confinement reserved for the innocent homebound.

And it is the story of a unique school we have built and what this school is doing and has done to lead these children out of darkness into day. Other communities have faced this problem of educating crippled children in a variety of ways. This book tells of our own moving experiences.

It is a story beset with unbelievable obstacles, difficulties, setbacks—and the grace of God that gave us the
strength to carry on, never to give up, for we were fighting
for something of great meaning: to give these children a
chance to learn to live, to lead full and joyful lives, including for some of them, marrying and having homes and
children of their own.

The purpose of liberal education for these children
about whom I have written is the same as for all children.
It should not be simply to adjust to the world as it is but
to remake it. Education and training are at their brightest
and most meaningful when used in the service of all men.

Many people of good will have believed in this cause
and assisted in this effort. In their work for these children
they place themselves in the ranks of those whom the
angels call God's friends.

There are so many to whom I am deeply grateful, not
only for their help in this struggle to bring to reality the
school that many said could never be, but also in the
preparation of this book about these children and this
warm personal adventure in which we all share. I thank
them with all my heart.

Henry Viscardi, Jr.

Albertson, L.I., N.Y.

Contents

Part I

THE HIDDEN CHILDREN

Part II

HOMEBOUND HOUSES

Part III

‖‖

READING, WRITING AND WHEELCHAIRS

Part IV

‖‖

BATTLEGROUND

The School

Part I

The Hidden Children

Chapter 1

‖‖

"Of course we feel sorry for them—how could anyone *not* feel sorry for children like that? . . . "

"It's simply that this school doesn't belong here, not right next door . . . it doesn't belong. . . . "

"Everyone agrees Mr. Viscardi is doing wonderful things for the handicapped. Everyone's grateful but . . . why not put this school in some lovely wooded area, some big estate off by itself?"

"Besides, these are homebound kids. Regular schools won't take them. Most of them never get inside a school. . . ."

"I mean it raises all kinds of problems but that doesn't mean we don't love them. . . . "

"Pity them? Of course. . . . "

"But right beside our own homes? Right outside our windows. . . . "

These were some of our neighbors talking, and their friends and supporters, in the corridors outside the Board of Zoning Appeals hearing room at the North Hempstead

Town Hall on Long Island, New York, in the early spring of 1964.

They were here to protest a variance we were seeking from the Zoning Board so that we could construct a school building unlike any school ever built, a school designed for children in wheelchairs, on litters, children who cannot walk normally or live normally, the severely disabled children who never go to school at all.

Many of these protesters were themselves mothers, fortunately of children who were whole and normal; they did not have to worry that their children might be doomed to live prisoned lives, needlessly buried away from the sight and prejudice of the world.

What was this school we already had in operation in its temporary quarters, this school for which we had raised more than three-quarters of a million dollars for a unique new building, with groundbreaking scheduled within weeks?

Who were these hidden homebound children, the pretty little girl with a steel hand and two artificial limbs, the handsome adolescent youth who walks on clumsy, eight-inch stumps? How had we ferreted them out of the shadows—and why?

In the first place these were homebound children whose only education was received from visiting teachers who came to their homes. These were not mentally retarded or emotionally disturbed children, but physically disabled solely. This was not to be a boarding school where such children could be sent but a day school to which they could travel by bus like any child. It was not merely a day care center but a real school with a sound and rounded educational program from kindergarten through high school. It would teach science and mathematics and languages. It would seek to demonstrate to the world that such children as we are talking about—the really severely disabled—should not be educationally deprived.

Naomi is an example. Naomi is sixteen years old, a lovely girl with a glorious, triumphant smile and wide expressive blue eyes. She loves music; she loves especially to listen to arias from *Madame Butterfly*. But Naomi's twisted little body is paralyzed; she spends her life on a litter, a reclining wheelchair. Her hands are contracted and with very little movement; only with great effort can she hold a book or turn a page or draw or write.

Yet Naomi participated in an unusual way at one of our directors' meetings. We have a tradition of warmth and informality at the board meetings. We serve a buffet luncheon; we invite many friends and individuals interested in the disabled in various ways. We present our reports on our activities and discuss our plans for the future. It was at one of these meetings, a day or two before Thanksgiving, that Naomi read to the Board and an assembly of parents, teachers and students an account she had written of the Pilgrims and the hardships they had endured in their first winter in America, how they had survived and how the harvest of the next summer was good and so they had set aside this day to give their thanks to God.

Naomi read this in her still small voice and you couldn't hear another sound in the room. Many of those parents had tears in their eyes. With all the young person's typical lack of self-consciousness, Naomi didn't realize how beautiful that reading was.

"Isn't it strange," she told me afterwards, "how many people were crying—they felt so sorry for the Pilgrims!"

Naomi is typical of the severely disabled homebound children who never get out of the front door, who often don't have a dress to wear because they never get dressed, who live from one day to the next as prisoners in their own home. A teacher comes once a week, perhaps twice. That is their education; that teacher is the whole outside world. These are children with normal minds. Their problem is physical disability.

Throughout our community, any community, our nation, in our so-called modern era of enlightenment, there are uncounted thousands of these hidden disabled children, backroom children the world seldom sees or guesses about. In the United States their number may run close to half a million. Prejudice, ignorance, superstition, fear all play their part in this strange conspiracy of silence. It's something you don't talk about, don't look at, don't think about.

True, the average school district has so very much with which to be concerned in its normal everyday activities. There are the thousands of normal children, the PTA, school taxes, transportation. After all, in each district severely disabled children represent only a small handful compared to the total number.

True, there are difficulties to have them in regular schools—for them and for the others. And there are stairs to climb, and crowded corridors. And who is there to help a child who is incontinent of bladder or bowel control, or one who is on a litter?

There are rehabilitation and training centers for such children. But after the rehabilitation and training center— no school, only the visiting teacher. None of the rich exposure to other children and the life of a school child; none of the stimulation and enrichment of a full academic experience.

Was there nothing that could be done for them? Was the fact that their legs and arms were twisted, that they were in wheelchairs, on litters—was this enough to deny them the normal experience of school life, to condemn them, to deny that any dream or aspiration they, like any child, might have would have no chance at all of fulfillment? Were they really different or the same as other children?

This was the reason for the school.

Our school was designed as a pilot operation, to serve as a continuing and growing demonstration to other communities of the nation in developing a meaningful program for children who might otherwise experience only limited educational development—if any at all.

"For the past two years," one of our reports to the Federal government declared, "the research and educational staff has worked on preliminary curriculum adaptation studies, teaching and parent orientation. . . . The staff has also conducted preliminary evaluations. . . .

"These preliminary and limited evaluations indicate that changes have occurred in the children. There are positive signs of academic achievement and marked improvement in social sophistication and physical growth. . . . The proposed demonstration . . . will attempt to show that disabled children who were previously homebound need not be so confined. . . ."

The night after the Zoning Board hearing I lay awake in the darkness of my bedroom a long time. Why had they allowed the postponement so that the opposition might bring in more witnesses to testify against us?

I was deeply concerned. What the Board did, how they voted on this matter, could do great harm, could come close to destroying all we had worked for. The future of the school was in grave peril. And strangely my own life and world and past seemed equally involved and indeed at stake.

Beside me in her bed my wife lay asleep. My four delightful daughters were asleep in their own rooms. It would seem I had everything I could want. Yet that night I could not sleep. For I was really nothing unless the cause for which I had fought and given so many years meant more than mere casual rejection, a mere brushoff by the community.

I was a man born without legs, from the rugged upper West Side, of emigrant Italian parentage. The first six years of my life I spent in hospitals, where I had more operations than I knew how to count. What should have been my legs were half-formed deformities, stumps, like somebody's unfinished statue.

On these stumps I fought my way up from the city streets. I learned to battle against the street gang taunts of "Ape Man, Ape Man, lookit the Ape Man."

When I finally did get out of hospitals and was sent to school, I remember my first day. The kids beat me up. They blackened my eye. They tore off my pants and cried out, "Let's see if he is like other men, this Ape Man."

It wasn't a pleasant memory, my first day in school. It was a terrible thing and there were many more days like it to follow.

Thinking back, years later, in the silence of my home, moments and meaning were sharply etched in my thoughts. Going on to school and college—Fordham— because I could ambulate; stumps or no stumps, I got up and down the stairs.

After college—I met a wonderful physician and lifelong associate, Dr. Robert Yanover, who told me he knew a Third Avenue legmaker who could make legs for me where others said it could not be done.

And I found myself standing, for the first time, on my artificial limbs, full grown, no longer an Ape Man three feet eight inches high.

I went on in business. I became personnel director for the great textile firm of Burlington Mills. I had a lovely wife and daughters; I had no need to return to the field of rehabilitation for the disabled.

But I did return to that work at the urging of Dr. Howard Rusk, whose institute of rehabilitation has become world famous, and of Bernard Baruch and the late Mrs. Roosevelt. I was the first director of the job-getting operation called J.O.B.—Just One Break—getting jobs for disabled people for whom at that time the "No help wanted" sign was almost universal.

Later, on a shoestring and a dream, in a vacant garage in West Hempstead, L.I., we began Abilities, Inc.—a work center designed to demonstrate how the disabled could do a real job in industry—if anyone would give them the chance.

At Abilities you have to be physically disabled to get a job. Recently, because of President Kennedy's interest, we have included the mentally retarded. We took on—continue to take on—many types of jobs; manufacturing, assembling electronic components, putting together and wiring airplane sections for major aircraft companies. We have asked no favors because we are restoring men and women to a useful life. We bid competitively, sometimes we win, sometimes we lose; our legless, armless, handless men and women compete with the best in industry—a day's work for a day's pay.

We have grown to more than four hundred employees —men and women. We bought a large tract of land in Albertson, L.I., a village within the boundaries of the town of North Hempstead; here, where they had been planning

a shopping center, we built our Abilities building and parking area; we landscaped, we brought in trees and bushes.

Out of this came the Human Resources Foundation, to
study what was actually happening to our workers, what
psychological and physiological changes were occurring as
a result of their work; we developed new electronic "telemetering" equipment for testing how they reacted physically; we built on adjacent property the Human Resources
Building for research—a building with laboratories, conference halls, meeting rooms, study rooms, a specially designed gymnasium, medical rooms, a beautiful and specially designed swimming pool.

And out of this building, which served as its temporary
headquarters, came perhaps this greatest dream of all—
the school.

The Human Resources School, we called it. A school
where the severely disabled child would get a chance to
meet life on realistic terms, where each child could have
the fullest opportunity to learn, to grow, to build his future, so that many of the heartbreaks our own workers at
Abilities had lived through might be avoided, many delays
and pitfalls and setbacks could be bypassed, so that the
severely crippled child of today could be—insofar as
humanly possible—the successful, accepted adult citizen
of tomorrow.

It was as if we were starting on a strange adventure into
an invisible jungle. Somewhere out there were children
who wanted to live, whose parents wanted them to live, to
enjoy life, to share in it, to have some measure of fulfill-

ment. And—as those of us who are severely disabled learned by the hard bitter route, *the world rejected them and still rejects them in many unthinking ways.* But these were the very children with whom we were concerned in our school. These were the boys and girls we wanted to bring into the light of everyday living, to the simple joy of being a full-fledged part of the world into which they were born.

Sometime after we launched our school operation I had a letter from the mother of one of our children. It described some of the problems she had been dealing with, the changes the school and its associations had brought about:

But there is a plus side to this too and here are some of the things we've been happily exposed to:

Last summer on a shopping trip the girls loaded crutches and wheelchairs into our station wagon and off for the department store in Hempstead we went. The conversation in the back seat went something like this: "Watch yourself girls, and brace yourselves for the furtive looks when suddenly some little kid will dart out and shout in a loud clear voice, 'Mummie, look at the big kid in the baby carriage.' And a red-faced mother will drag him away by the ear, admonishing him never to do a thing like that again."

These were the girls talking among themselves and laughing about it—if you just listened to the laughter in the back of that car you would think it was active undisabled teenagers out for a riotous time . . .

Just a year ago these children were lost, frustrated, completely discouraged. What has happened since then has changed their lives. They're accepted. They're people. And pity plays no part.

This was the goal: To bring youngsters like these out of the shadows, to give them purpose, direction, meaning, achievable goals, realistic goals, destinies they could forge, skills they could learn, meanings they could make real.

We had purchased extra land, we had ample grounds on which to build this school adjacent to Abilities, where the children could see and mingle with the world, could have the object lesson of people even more disabled than they themselves, severely disabled men and women leading exciting, productive, happy and useful lives, earning a good living, driving cars, owning homes, marrying, raising families, supporting themselves.

Not tucked away unseen in some wooded area, some private estate, some no man's land.

In the darkness, in the silence of that night, I knew why this was important, the outcome of this issue. For this was the old battle, summed up, the same battle all of us had been fighting all of our lives. The objection was not to the school but to the students who would attend, crippled, unpleasant to look upon.

Perhaps I overemphasized the meaning, but I did not think so. For it was a symbol, this particular suburban battle. It had to be fought out. A precedent had to be set, established. Was the world to be divided into able and disabled people, the blessed and the damned?

To me it seemed the lives and destinies and futures of tens of thousands of these children would depend on the decision reached in this obscure zoning board hearing room in the North Hempstead town hall of a place called Manhasset, Long Island, N.Y.

We already had a school in operation in temporary quarters at the Human Resources Building. We were already achieving results with these homebound children who had never gone to school. But unless we had our own building with its specially designed facilities and teaching techniques, many more could not be accommodated, no truly meaningful demonstration project for the world to see could be possible.

And it was precisely this projected new building we had designed with such care—the dream school for the hidden disabled youngsters of the world—that the neighbors so strongly opposed.

They loved these children, of course—they all agreed on that. They wanted all the best for these kids, every possible break. Their lawyer, even as he argued strongly against the variance before the Zoning Board, insisted on this fact again and again. They too wanted these children to have every opportunity to live and learn like other children, like their own children.

Only not here.

Chapter 2

||||||||||||||||||||||||||||||||||||||||||||||||||||||||||||||||||

It began on a night in very early spring, 1961. The Human Resources Building was very close to completion. We had many discussions as to how we could most effectively use our new research facility. Much of the actual research and recreational activities would come with our own people after the end of their working day at Abilities. During the day some of the study areas and large meeting rooms, even the swimming pool itself, would be unused.

We were meeting in my office at Abilities. Ellen was there, that night, my dark-haired assistant who had been with us almost since Abilities was founded. Ellen was paralyzed by polio at twelve. She has since married and has children of her own and is busy as mother and house-wife in California. Art Nierenberg was there too—our plant manager, also paralyzed and in a chair; Frank Gentile, another of our executives; and Alex, our legless, armless foreman of the packaging department.

Each of us had our memories, our battles, our victories and defeats.

"I wasn't homebound, Hank," Alex was saying. "I

didn't know enough to stay home. In Brooklyn the gangs are tough. The kids would pick me up and throw me into the drink—the ocean, that is. So I learned how to swim or I would of drowned. . . . "

Alex makes a joke out of the battles and the victories. The next moment he was talking about when he was adult and alone in a rented room and had no idea of what to do, where to go for a job—not a handout but work.

"I made dates to kill myself. I'd say to myself, 'Next Tuesday—if you don't get a job of some kind by then . . . ' but next Tuesday would come and I would make some excuse to put it off. I'd give life one more chance."

It was lucky he did because one day he heard about Abilities and came out to see me and that night I sent him a telegram telling him to report for work in the morning.

We talked that spring evening about these personal episodes. Ellen, recalling the fact that she was homebound for some years, reminded us, "It's all a question of who's your homebound teacher—what she's like."

"It's so confining to any youngster—any ambitious youngster—who finds himself pent up, immobile, useless. The friends you had before you were disabled drift off— you don't see them. The only contact you have with the outside world is probably that homebound teacher."

"And you didn't get out at all?"

"I had those heavy braces on both legs. We lived on the fifth floor and it was a walkup. I didn't get out, almost not at all. I can still see myself sitting at the kitchen table with some home instruction teacher. It was O.K. if you had a nice one. One I had for two years actually became like a member of the family and we're still in touch with her. She was dedicated; she wanted nothing better than to bring education, warmth, understanding and companionship into the lives of her pupils.

"But, boy, I remember another teacher I had for one year. She was a Grade A witch and take my word for it—I'm spelling it wrong. She was annoyed because we lived on the fifth floor and she had to walk up those stairs. She was annoyed!

Ellen's eyes flashed as she told this story—full of Irish anger but also mixed in with her Irish humor.

"She didn't care about me at all," Ellen said slowly. "She wasn't there for that reason. She was doing this job because it paid well and wasn't too demanding. Can you imagine if this was the only education I was ever to have —waiting for her arrival three times a week, one and a half hours each time. That's it, little girl. Live it up!"

"We all had it, one way or another," Art commented. "As children, as adults . . . "

"The homebound child has it the worst," Ellen persisted. "How can he or she learn to live, learn to face anything, locked up like a criminal in his own home?"

The school on that night in 1961 was only a germ in my mind, a possibility that one day would take form but about which I spoke very little to anyone.

We began to talk and think about children. We called up in our minds our own memories, the jolts of growing up and realizing what lay ahead, the boundaries of reality we had to face, the prejudice, the averted eyes you had to learn to understand.

Out there in the early spring, I thought—children, children who were just as we had been, or worse, children with all the pent up loneliness of the homebound, all the useless, meaningless dreams.

We talked of these children and of ourselves. Ellen recited one camping experience she had and how the program seemed to be given over to sports that proved just what a crippled child *couldn't* do. "I refused to take any part in sports that did that," Ellen flared.

"What about a summer camp—intelligently planned for children severely disabled?" I suggested. "Suppose we used our Human Resources Building, the grounds outside the bowling alley, the swimming pool—"

Ellen asked if I meant by this homebound children. I told her yes, the children who had nowhere else to go, no place to go because no regular summer camp program could take them.

Art wondered how we would find these kids. Ellen said, "Oh—we'll go to the Easter Seal Society, we'll knock on doors, beat the boondocks and the bushes. They're out there. Just as we were, Art."

Suddenly as we were talking I realized that we were about to start a summer camp for homebound children.

But what would happen to them at the end of the six weeks camping period. Would they go back then into their prisons?

The possibility of the school coming into being for these children began to take form in my thoughts . . .

The next morning I called Dick Switzer.

I must say a special word here about his extraordinary background because he plays a key role—as the man I picked to direct the summer camp and the man I intended from the start to be headmaster of the school.

Dick is himself disabled by cerebral palsy, but not too severely. This gives him an advantage in teaching other disabled people; he knows from firsthand experience some of their special difficulties, what goes on within them, their needs in dealing with a world that will not understand.

I first met him in a low point of his career—he had just failed all the educational courses he was taking in Industrial Art at Oswego State College. Dick is a tall man, over six feet. But he walks with a limp and movement of one hand is partially impaired. His speech is unimpaired. He happens also to be one of the most brilliant teachers of the young disabled that I have ever seen.

But in 1952—as an example of what all handicapped people, those with only a measure of disability, have to endure—he found himself suddenly flunked in courses at Oswego in which he knew he was doing honor work. His first semester had been all honor grades. Second semester —failure. Not in one subject or two—but in every course.

He hurried to the Dean's office for an explanation. The Dean informed him, "We don't think anyone with your handicap should be teaching industrial arts. With your bad hand we don't think you can teach children to use tools properly. We want you out of the Industrial Arts department."

Just like that. Compared to many others Dick is not a seriously handicapped person—but this is still the reaction, still the treatment meted out! He asked if he couldn't at least teach elementary school—teachers were needed, especially in Elementary Ed.

The answer was still no. This was the Easter vacation and Dick went home, apparently washed out. Faculty members of the college, however, knew the remarkable record Dick Switzer had been achieving, the talent he had displayed in summer teaching projects, and the outraged educators stormed into action for him with the Dean and other officials.

"Change him from industrial arts," they said, "but don't boot him out of the college with a record of failure in all his courses when he is, in fact, doing brilliant work."

Because of this concern for Dick's future, he did return to study elementary education.

It was during this period of indecision when he was likely to be thrown out because of his limp and one partially bad hand that he came to see me.

Abilities in 1952 was only a small plant in a remodelled garage in West Hempstead, Long Island. But Dick and I talked and he told me of the possibility of his returning to Oswego to study elementary education. Even then this idea of a school was taking shape. Here was the man who might play a part in it.

I told him: "You go back there and take that Elementary Ed course and finish it. Take Physical Education courses too. You may need those. One day as part of the work we do in rehabilitation I'm going to build a swimming pool and perhaps—"

I remember the way Dick looked around at our cluttered remodeled garage, where a hundred industrial activities were going on at once, with none of the beautiful buildings or space we now have at our plant in Albertson, and I saw his bewildered expression, the vague doubt of my sanity.

"Oh, not here," I admitted. "But one day—when we have a plant of our own design. It'll be somewhere near. We're already thinking about how we can phase that big dream into reality."

That summer, while he was still preparing for his studies in Elementary Ed, I put him to work in our plant, on the wire harnesses and cable jobs we do for aircraft firms. It was the first time Dick had worked at this kind of job, and the first time he had worked with disabled people.

"This may be an important part of your preparation for the job you do for us when we start our school," I told him.

Dick shook his head in mild bewilderment.

That was almost ten years before the spring night when the idea of our camp first took shape. Dick had finished his education at Oswego. He had taught elementary school and taught the physically disabled children—not home-bound, however—in the Brentwood school district on Long Island. He had taken courses toward his master's degree in Special Education—education for the disabled—at Syracuse University. And he was married and support-ing his wife and two children.

But over the years we had kept in touch. And I called him about this new plan.

"I'm going to start a summer camp, Dick," I told him. "I want you to run it. Can you come over and let's talk about it?"

He was excited by the idea. Where was the camp to be? What kind of kids?

I didn't dare tell him over the phone. "Come on over here, Dick. Ellen and I will explain. We've got a big new building, we've got some grass and trees and a swimming pool so far without water. It's a great facility for young-sters."

"And where are the youngsters coming from?"

"We don't know, Dick. Not exactly. You better hurry over."

The problem of finding homebound youngsters who had no place to go in the summer months was not, we discov-ered, a difficult one.

The Easter Seal Society and the local Polio Foundation people were glad to be of help, particularly when they learned that our camp would be directed by Switzer who was a certified teacher for the disabled of all types and was working in this field of special education in the Brentwood school district.

The agencies were delighted at the prospect of opening up new vistas for children like these. They worked closely with Dick Switzer and Ellen in meeting with the parents and children to bring this beginning phase into reality.

There were about twelve children in all, half boys, half girls, all seriously disabled physically. For these children it would be like a midsummer dream come true.

Ages ranged from about eight to fifteen or sixteen—but it must be realized that because of the difficulty of these youngsters to grow or get education, ages in terms of time with the severely crippled are not always indicative of the rate of development, educationally, emotionally, physically, mentally.

Their intelligence was normal. They represented many types of physical disabilities—polio paraplegia, spina bifida, arthritis, blood dyscrasia, arthrogryposis, malformations of hands and limbs—a complete cross section of disability itself in the young.

One was a wonderful lad called Gil. This was a spina bifida case. Due to lack of fusion of the vertebrae and maldevelopment of the spinal cord one of the results is incontinence of bladder. This caused constant dribbling of urine and inadequate emptying of his bladder. You had to rub his tummy and apply pressure to the bladder area to enable him to relieve himself.

From his earliest infancy, his mother had tended him and his special needs. When Switzer and Ellen talked with her, she was delighted at the fact that Gil could go to camp despite his problem that had kept him out of so many normal activities throughout his life.

But she would have to be there, she explained to Dick, to take care of Gil's special toilet problem.

Dick did not challenge her suggested arrangement at that time. But Ellen later told me, "There was something in Dick's expression . . ."

She was right. Three days after camp began, following a discussion with Dick, I told Gil's mother, "There's a nurse here as well as Mr. Switzer and myself—we can take care of your boy—we urge you not to come. Give him a little sense of breaking parental dependency."

Reluctantly, I think, she accepted the plan.

It was the first time she had been away from him in this way.

Two weeks later, Dick took one extra step: Gil was in the locker room getting ready to go into the pool. He was eager to get in and he was waiting impatiently for Dick to take care of him. He would have to be toileted before swimming.

But Dick deliberately decided he had business in some other part of the building. Gil was left alone, wanting desperately to join the others already in the pool. Every minute he waited was one less minute in the pool. All his life he had been in the care of someone else. Now Gil stretched out on a locker bench and took care of his needs as he had observed others do so many times.

Relieved, he climbed into his wheelchair and headed

after the others. When Dick returned the boy was in the pool swimming and waving a victorious hand in the general direction of Mr. Switzer.

He took care of himself thereafter.

We first met brown-eyed Joan that summer too. When Joan was younger she had been hospitalized and many people said she would never even sit up. A pretty girl, too seriously paralyzed to be accepted in regular school, she had been on homebound instruction for three years.

When we first talked about this phase of Joan's life, her mother told me, "They so desperately need education, homebound children, they're like vegetables, they can't move about, but if you complain that won't change it—no one really seems to care."

The homebound teacher was a good one, the mother told us, but her regular work was as a substitute teacher, and she would have to shift her time around when she was needed to fill in for an absent regular teacher in school, and she would call up and say, "Tell Joan I can't be there today at nine this morning—I'll come in at six this evening." It wasn't her fault; that was the way it was.

"And many times Joan would be having her lesson while I was trying to feed the rest of the family. And all this was bad for Joan because children need a certain discipline in their lives and many times she would not see the teacher for three or four days, maybe in one week she would have one and then the following week make up the lost time. There was no routine, no range of studies, no foreign language or music or—any of that."

"We wrote to people, we contacted people in the local area, we pleaded with them to get us more than an hour a day for Joan. We couldn't afford a private tutor ourselves. But no one—no one could do anything. And here was another summer of nothing but shut-in frustration.

"Should we take her outside to sit alone in a wheelchair, with other children turning from her, scorning her, or making remarks that children—not realizing what the hurt is—often do?"

Far off I seemed to hear—with a faint bitter overtone —words out of long ago: "Ape Man! Ape Man!"

"So you can see," Joan's mother was saying, "what it meant when I received a letter telling me that there was going to be a summer camp and that she could go if we could provide transportation. A summer camp for severely handicapped children—as Joan certainly is.

"Doctors at the Hospital for Special Surgery told us that Joan must have another operation in the fall, to give her more movement in one arm. But, they said, why not let her have this summer camping experience first."

She spent so much time in the pool that summer, giving her arm so much exercise, that at the end of the six-week period, the doctors at the Hospital for Special Surgery found the arm so greatly improved and mobility so greatly increased through her swimming that surgery was no longer necessary or indicated.

Another part of the story I learned later from Joan's

mother. She told me, many months later, "You know, we think of you and your school as a real miracle for us. You see, we went to Lourdes, we were so concerned about Joan and what was happening; we went and we prayed to Our Lady of Lourdes there that Joan might get a chance to live her life fully and wholly."

Only a little after that, she said, when they were back in America, the letter came telling her about the camp we were starting, and the real possibility that Joan could attend with other children. This was what they had prayed for . . .

And beyond the camp—although none of us realized it at the time, or knew the problems that would be encountered on the way—was the school.

As the day of starting the camp grew closer, there was an increase in general hectic activity. Dick and Frank Gentile and I and others were putting together a staff. We had one or two volunteers, a one-armed teacher handled the arts and crafts program; she had only recently graduated from college and obtained her teaching license; we were later able to help her in obtaining a full-time teaching job, despite her disability, in the New York Public Schools. We had one swimming instructor, Jill Rockwell, who did excellently but who was put out of action for a day or so when one of our disabled children batted a pitched ball into her left eye.

Camp was about to begin. We were meeting with the parents of these children, talking out problems, quieting fears and concerns, talking about car pools and transportation and safety rules, lunches, bathing togs, problems and techniques for toileting youngsters who could not handle their own needs.

It was a beginning, an exciting, challenging, exhilarating moment.

Chapter 3

Twelve children—on crutches and in wheelchairs—around a flagpole in the morning sun.

I stood and watched from my office window. Watched and listened to this hodgepodge pickup team of the young disabled; twelve children saluting the flag, even one of them helping Camp Director Dick Switzer in the flag-raising ceremony.

Twelve disabled kids singing in varied pitches and at assorted age levels, "Oh, say can you see, By the dawn's early light, What so proudly we hailed . . ."

This is the kind of thing you can't put into words, what it meant to watch these children, so unconscious of themselves in that moment, so concerned with all the ceremony, with the flag itself, the salute.

Camp began each morning this way, after the kids piled out of the cars that brought them in the parents' car pool setup, and the wheelchairs were set up and the parents waved their farewells and left their charges with us.

Sometimes I would go out and join them, and joke and chat after the ceremony itself was over. I have never, from the start, made any attempt to hide my own feeling for these kids.

I'm the biggest sentimentalist of all, I think. Or close to it. I've lived with disability myself and I conquered it and made a place for myself, and I've worked with other people, with Dr. Rusk and his institute, I started Abilities—all of this.

I know they don't want my pity—and they don't get it either. I know they want real help in helping themselves, and I'll give them that too, with all the professional techniques we can find.

I guess my personal reaction comes because they're so young; because they still have the big unsullied highway of unlimited hopes in front of them; the world is wonderful when you're a kid, able or disabled. To be a child is a pretty wonderful thing. It's nothing for a child to think in terms of riding a rocket to the moon. Most of us grownup mature leaders wouldn't think such a thing as feasible for us but a child would; they've got the great capacity of changing mice into horses and pumpkins into jet planes. Nothing into everything.

But they couldn't do it all by themselves. The rest of us had to help. We had to give them the start and this camp was where it began. I thought watching them that first morning, this collection of youngsters in a circle with this big, lumbering, awkward-gaited, driving, dedicated Dick Switzer leading the kids in a salute to the flag in the morning sun, on the lawn outside the windows of Abilities, Inc., and our new Human Resources Building across the path—it was then that I knew beyond any question that the school had to be. These children weren't just a theory—they were a fact. A fact of life—our lives, all lives—of people who care. They were with us, part of us.

I knew in that moment one inescapable fact: I dared not let go of what we had begun for children like these.

There was much we didn't know—it was an experiment, we recognized. A grant for $1,000 helped defray some of the expenses, for equipment, games, balls, quoits, assorted supplies. Transportation we purposely left to the parents. We told them, "Look, we're here and your child can have all the benefits we have to offer, including lunch, but you must face the problem of getting him here and home." So they all met and worked out the schedules. The timetables were kept a lot better than the schedules of the Long Island Railroad.

Dick worked out the camp curriculum. With his training in Special Education, plus the fact that as a youth he had himself been a real camper, he evolved a program that blended realism and practicability with adventure and meaning—in terms of what these children thought of as adventure.

We even talked with our children about the events and what we were going to do—and what they wanted to do.

"A picnic—can we go on a picnic?"

And Dick would ask them, "All right—what's a picnic? What do you do on a picnic?"

"Well, you have a fire, somebody cooks, you eat things. You eat hot dogs."

One of our boys—Peter—was very upset about this. He

was one who had been homebound almost entirely; he had never had a hot dog on a roll. He thought we were talking about eating an actual dog.

Dick explained to him that it was just a frankfurter on a roll—with mustard.

I don't think he understood until we did go on an actual picnic at a Jesuit retreat house only a few miles from us.

According to the reports, Peter ate more hot dogs than anyone on the trip.

We had a young woman as lifeguard who could swim like a dolphin, and we had another volunteer who helped in physical education and training, especially in the pool and swimming. Dick knitted this program together—the arts and crafts, the swimming, the gym, games and sports; he knew from his own experience as well as training the needs and the balanced program that would give them satisfaction and achievement without too great a challenge or physical load.

In the arts and crafts they had a lot of "projects" not unlike what they have in all camps and schools. I know my own daughters brought home a pair of book ends which, based on the overall expenses of the camping experience during which they were made, cost me a mere $415.

Still the projects at this camp had a slight difference; practically none of these children had ever tried to make anything truly on their own like this.

One of the boys started in on a battleship. That's quite a challenge even for normal kids who can get around all they want.

He started in on it with high hopes, everybody putting in his advice, suggestions and occasionally his active participation.

But this was a real camp, and they didn't just sit around on these projects on our grounds; part of the learning to which Dick Switzer is dedicated is moving out, seeing the new things, trying new avenues. Particularly with these children.

Wheelchairs and crutches notwithstanding, the children went on field trips. We took them, for example, to one large Long Island estate to see the beautiful gardens. Some of our campers had never been in a garden, had never seen flowers cultivated and growing like this. Dick also took them to the Bronx Zoological Gardens. This was, I gathered, a rather typical trip of a young class to the zoo. I did hear that one of our children fell in love with a particularly arrogant ostrich. And another reportedly asked one of the guards in the monkey house, "What do gorillas do if they have to have wheelchairs?" I never learned the answer.

Perhaps the most extraordinary of all those adventures that first summer was the junket on the yacht.

Several of the children, I discovered, lived near the water and had been making hints: Could we take a camping trip on a boat—maybe on a yacht? A real yacht like the ones they show on television?

This one Dick passed along to me. I called a distinguished member of our advisory board at Abilities, Charles Valentine, owner of one of the largest tugboat lines in New York City. If anyone could tell me how to find a spare yacht, it was Valentine. I put it just that way: "Charles, do you happen to know anybody with a yacht he's not using in the middle of the week?"

After a long pause, he said, "Hank, what do you want a yacht for?"

I explained about the camp and the kids.

There was another long pause. Then he said, "Let me look around and I'll call you back."

Half an hour later he called back: and gave me the name of a boat.

He gave me the name of a boat, the owner, the Captain, and the marina where the boat was tied up.

"Now listen, Hank. The owner has already called the Captain. The whole thing is set. The Captain has orders to take care of us—us means you and your kids—the minute you tell him. Okay?"

I said, "Charley, the kids will love you forever. I'll buy you a yacht to pay you back."

You get caught up in this kind of project with these children. I cut my work short the next day to get over to Port Washington and I found the boat he was talking about—it was moored in the marina—a beautiful, spacious seventy-foot yacht with all the trimmings.

I went on board, presented myself to the Captain. The instant he realized who I was he snapped to attention. "Well, Sir," he said, "where do you want to go and when? My orders are to put on board all the food you need and all the Cokes and take you and the children wherever you want to go."

One week later our young wanderlust brigade—most of whom had never been on board a boat before—made the grand circuit tour of Manhattan Island on that luxury yacht. They ate hot dogs and hamburgs and drank Cokes and saw the sights of the greatest city in the world.

We drove the kids out in private cars and the company station wagon. The gangway was a difficult maneuver and most of the youngsters we carried aboard. The reaction of those children was sheer bug-eyed wonder. This was a real plush yacht with ship-to-shore radio and telephone, cushioned chairs and spacious cabins and staterooms below— of course they were somewhat inaccessible to the kids because the companionways were narrow and steep.

We all sat out on the stern which was large and had plenty of chairs and was shaded from the sun with canvas but you could see everything. We moved out across the waters of Manhasset Bay and through the Hellgate Passage. There ahead of us was Manhattan; some of the youngsters had never seen that skyline; they'd lived in New York or close to it but had never seen Manhattan.

For the first time they were seeing the world. They were looking at it with wide open eyes, looking at this city of soaring buildings, this world of bridges and ships and cars that sped along the East River Drive and across the bridges themselves, this vibrating universe of which, with immediate reality, they were now a part.

We came down the East River, past the millionaire apartment houses of Sutton Place, the Brooklyn Navy Yard and Wall Street, the Battery, the Statue of Liberty,

up the Hudson River past the great blackhulled red-funnel
liners, past Grant's Tomb and the Riverside Church and
Palisades Amusement Park and the George Washington
Bridge, into the Harlem River and past Yankee Stadium,
the Hellgate Passage on our way home.

They stood at the rails and they munched their hot dogs
and rolls and they watched the world with a glorious participation in their eyes.

During the first summer changes occurred in our children, even in these few weeks. By the end of the six-week
period there was a whole new air of freedom, of release, of
delight in what they could do; mothers called us to say that
their children were more independent, wanted to do more
on their own, were acting more like typical teen-agers,
even talking for hours on the phone. "Florence is forever
on the phone with Maria, hour after hour."

Dick tried to explain that it was normal—and all to the
good.

But while there were these changes in individuals, there
remained the problem of the future—the tomorrow that
was swiftly approaching. A few of our children would be
returning to regular schoolrooms to try to compete despite
severe disabilities.

Most of the others would be going back on homebound
instruction. To private prisons, to one-hour a day of a
learning experience, isolated from all other children. It is
hard to know when a child will be accepted or rejected; he
may go through the first eight grades, only to find himself

rejected for high school and shunted back to the four walls. It may occur sooner.

These were the problems facing us, facing our children, as summer drew to its close.

I was aware of how much it had meant to them, almost without their realizing it. We had already begun efforts to start a school; we were already running into great difficulties. And we already knew that we could not and would not let these children or their parents settle for second-rate lives.

The gratitude of the parents for the help, the care, the fact that someone had done something beyond the bare legal requirements, was evident in words and action.

One day from my office windows at Abilities I saw a woman on her knees on the lawn; she was busy pulling up dandelions, crabgrass and weeds. I had seen this performance before; I recognized the woman as one of our camp mothers.

I went out to chat with her. She looked up, saw me, understood my questioning expression I suppose, and said quickly, "How else can I show you how much I feel about what you've done for my little girl? At least I can clean out the weeds on the lawn."

I told her, "Why, we haven't even begun to do all we can. We're going to get a real school for her, with all the things it should have in it, everything on one floor, ramps instead of stairways, classrooms especially designed, libraries . . ."

So out of the first summer's exposure to these kids—and they to us—on this experimental basis, came our determination to provide the school, the real future, a real educational program for the severely disabled.

We had an exciting camp graduation. Everyone on the staff and all the kids were emotionally involved. The parents were there for the ceremony. Some had misty eyes. Several wept quite openly.

There was no reason for weeping because it was a pretty gay closing-of-camp-for-the-season kind of exercise. The boys presented me with a gift—the model battleship they had been working on with Dick Switzer's help. There were rumors that the boys talked one of our top wirers at Abilities into lending a hand with more difficult wiring but into this aspect of the matter I never dared to inquire. It was a fine battleship. I accepted it with great pride.

I gave them a little talk, too. Those closing moments were tape recorded. Some of the excerpts with the youngsters reveal, I think, attitudes, problems, fears and dreams we all shared about the future.

That final day they sat around me under a shade tree and we talked about what they wanted to be—in the future —when they were grown up. A teacher . . . a priest . . . an astronaut. We laughed and joked. And then I talked more seriously to them, pointing out some of the facts of life that had to be faced above all others.

"I remember when I was a boy," I said, "I was born without legs, you know. These are artificial limbs that I wear but I didn't have them when I was a boy. And I spent my time when I wasn't in hospitals on the streets of New York's West side, and getting about on the stumps.

"I'm going swimming with you later and you're going to see my stumps, what they look like without my limbs on. I remember that I grew up in a world where there were problems of being accepted, problems of whether I could become a priest if I wanted to become a priest. I did think I wanted to be a priest once but I found out as I grew older that I couldn't because I was disabled. I wasn't sure I wanted to be anyway, but I thought of it. I didn't think of being a teacher but I sure loved college, the years I spent at Fordham University as a student.

"But I soon realized, as I got older, that when you're disabled, when you get around on crutches, or braces, wheelchairs, when you have something different in your life, the world doesn't accept you as readily.

"When I asked you all to come here and spend a delightful summer I had in mind that we could show you that there was a future, although it might not involve being astronauts—I hear they have some pretty rigid requirements physically on the boys they put into the capsules. I think it could involve being a teacher . . . but it might not be pitching for the New York Yankees—as I used to dream of doing—or becoming chief of police or some of the other things in the world that we know—realistically— we can't do.

"I had in mind a rather latent purpose in asking you to come and spend the summer with us. In Abilities we have a lot of disabled people who are making their way in the world, marrying and buying homes and driving cars and having children—in spite of the fact that they are disabled and are considered different from the rest of the world.

"You know we have some four hundred people like that, working right here—you've seen them and talked with them. These are our people who have learned to live with what they have left and to make a real go of it. They might not have been accepted as astronauts or priests, yet they find a happy life, someone who loves them, someone who can share their happiness. They know children and homes and families of their own—of your own when you grow up."

And I talked then about our plans for a school, and would they like it and what would they like most to learn. One voice cried out, "It would be great to have all games —but leave out the arithmetic." But they favored courses in learning how to live, how to get along with people. . . .

They were serious about it, though, and asked many questions and made several extremely interesting comments. Most of all they wanted to know when it was going to open, this school we planned. Would it be sometime soon, sometime in the fall?

And they wanted to know when were we going to have lunch.

Chapter 4

So far as our immediate plans for starting a pilot school were concerned, a demonstration of what could be done in special classrooms outside the home, my enthusiasm was a bitter miscalculation.

We did not know the dimensions. The extent of the need we only guessed. Yet almost before the summer camp was in full swing, we were talking about the school we wanted to open in the fall. For once it was I who let enthusiasm run ahead of reality.

Carried away by the exuberance of the camp, I had almost come to believe that everyone stood ready to help such children; no one would seriously try to impede any program that was serious, that would provide facilities, and bring in top professional teachers and staff.

I had totally underestimated the pitfalls, the fixed attitudes, the roadblocks, the suspicion of our motives—the walls of fear and silence that many parents and doctors, disappointed by past promise and hope, fling up around the homes of the severely disabled youngster.

Our camp operation had found these children quickly

through the local agencies. It was a program of only six weeks in the summer. It presented no great problem to officials, bureaus or individuals.

But a school? A full-time school for children everybody had already said couldn't go to school? That presented a whole new issue.

In our files at Abilities, we have the record of hundreds of workers whose replies to the question regarding education on their original application reads: "No formal education. On homebound ed." These are men and women now holding down difficult and demanding jobs with us.

Forty percent of our employees fall into that category: *No formal schooling. Homebound.*

Even as the camp program was taking shape, I began to make the first forays into the question of the school.

I talked about this concept of mine with one of my good friends and associates, William Spinelli of the New York State Division of Vocational Rehabilitation. I said, "Here's a tragic situation, Bill. These kids can come to our place and enjoy themselves—but they can't go to school, most of them. Why not? I want to start a school for this kind of child."

We talked about the homebound situation and its shortcomings. We discussed the difficulty of getting information, a foothold of facts.

Bill Spinelli said, "Let me look into it. There are records and some of the information is available. Types of disabilities, degrees of ambulatory effectiveness, the physical, emotional, mental status . . ."

The facts he provided gave us a start. They indicated that there were, in every school district, a considerable number of disabled children, some going to school, some staying home.

These were general statistics and data of an incomplete nature, of course. To get the full story, to begin to see what children our facilities could serve, I put Ellen Bagatta and Bill Campbell, a young educator who was then working as a research associate for us at Abilities and Human Resources Foundation, on special assignment. Starting with Bill Spinelli's information, they were to talk with the school districts throughout the area. We would begin to get a real picture of where these children were to whom we could be of greatest service, the nucleus of students for this school.

It was here, as they began their phone calls and visits, that we ran into our first major roadblock.

The wall of silence suddenly loomed.

There were no facts. And if there were any, they were not available.

To prove a need for a school for such children, we had to prove that the children existed on a widespread basis— not just in one localized segment or section. We knew that all children supposedly had to be registered and those exempted from school and put on home education had to be certified as "too severely crippled" to go to school.

Exactly what this constituted was not always definable in precise terms. Each school district set up its own general rules and measurements. The severity of the disability was usually the measure—but also involved were such things as the stairs a child would have to climb up and down in his school, the extent of the disability in relation to the overall school program. Specific disabilities that could be involved in exemption ran from epilepsy, heart conditions, rheumatic fever, muscular dystrophy and polio to rare paralytic disorders, physical malformation, retardation, inability to adjust emotionally.

What Ellen and Bill were attempting to get were figures on the individual districts in regard to homebound teaching, the number of students available if we could set up a school where they could get more education than the homebound method of a few hours a week provided. From census figures we had indications of large numbers—the total figure for Long Island alone, for example, would indicate hundreds of disabled children of school age either on homebound education—or getting none at all.

But around these questions was a great deal of information which we could not readily obtain.

Many of the schools to which they came could not provide the individual who had this information. No information was available; no such children in their districts, that they knew of. School officials told them, "You're on a wild child chase. We have no homebound cases in this community."

Some said they knew of no disabled children in their

schools—or in their communities—although Ellen and Bill had been able, through other sources, to get records showing instances of disabled children in these very communities where school authorities insisted no such cases existed.

In some districts the official attitude was: This was a problem area and they were handling it as best they could; leave it alone. Outsiders were not invited to check up on what was or was not being done on behalf of these children.

One school official told Ellen bluntly, his tone hinting that crippled children involved top-secret security, "We are not allowed to give out that kind of information."

And he hung up.

Both Ellen and Bill were careful to explain—wherever they got the chance—who they were and whom they represented. Ellen, of course, was herself in a wheelchair when she made personal calls.

One official informed Bill, "Not only will we not tell you how we handle this kind of educational situation—we want to especially inform you that this is not your business. We'll not let outsiders butt in on these children."

One could find a thousand reasons for this attitude. Who were we to go barging in on this problem? We weren't educators. Disabled or not, what right did we have to try to tell them how to do their jobs?

But there were some also who understood.

One was a nurse in a large school district within the county. She went far beyond the call of duty in helping

Ellen and Bill Campbell to put together a picture of some of the homebound cases.

A director of personnel in another school district in the county, and a research worker in still another, provided data on children on homebound instruction, who could, in our opinion, attend the kind of school we were planning.

That lovely nurse filled us in with special facts and details. Many cases, as we well knew, never were reported to her, but she knew of them in one way or another—from parents who educate their children themselves, and do not report details to authorities.

"There is a little spina bifida girl—that is where the backbone is not fully formed, there is a separation and incontinence . . ." the nurse explained. "But there are ways the problem could be handled, you know . . . so that if someone wanted to take the trouble to solve this . . ."

There always had to be someone willing to take the trouble.

And she began to tell them of another child, a ten-year-old boy with arthrogryposis—a congenital immobility of the joints of upper and lower extremities.

In all, despite the obstacles, they were finally able to obtain from three cooperating school districts a total sampling of twelve cases. All homebound children. All on extremely limited homebound education of a few hours a week or less.

Twelve cases—the facts grudgingly given by the community out of the shadows. A fragmentary sampling only, although the data on each of the cases we had was complete. Each of the children would be perfectly capable, we could demonstrate, to attend not any ordinary school—but the kind of school we envisioned.

And statistically the facts indicated that there must be hundreds more, in every school district in the county, in every county.

This was the essential point we had to present at that time: That the condition existed, the children were being shunted into a medieval isolation, their education was totally inadequate.

Something, some way had to be found, to bring these prisoners out of that nothingness into daylight.

Shortly after we had begun to put together these preliminary facts, a meeting was held in Albany at the New York State Education Department Bureau for Handicapped Children. Present were several friends of ours—our own Bill Campbell, who was shortly to leave us to join the Hicksville School District research staff; Marvin Gibson, a distinguished educator and director of personnel in that school district, and the district's assistant superintendent of schools.

They had gone there for other school purposes but were able to discuss with the man who directed most of the programming for disabled children the problem we had been working on, this half-forgotten world of the homebound child and his education.

They reported to him my firm belief that most of these children should, in fact, be going to school.

It was, admittedly, a revolutionary concept.

I didn't know Ray Simches then but I was to later. He was to tell me, one day, of his concern at that first meeting. For ten years in that department he had worked to utilize the availability of homebound instruction for physically disabled children as a technique to educate them since these children could not attend public schools. Now suddenly he was informed that—according to Henry Viscardi—such children were able to be in school.

Simches responded by challenging Gibson, "If it's true, why haven't you and other school districts brought it up before? In all the years, you've never said you thought these children on home instruction could be in school instead. You send documents with statements from physicians stating that this child is physically unable to attend school. Otherwise we wouldn't approve the child for home instruction."

It was logical that Ray Simches, a dedicated educator, should have deep reservations about the whole thing. On the other hand, if what they were saying to him had an element of truth, he could not in conscience turn from it. He suggested to them that if this was a real problem and Henry Viscardi knew all about it, then, as he put it, a meeting should be held with Mr. Viscardi "to discuss the nature of the problem, the extent of the problem, and possibly some solutions for coping with the problem.

When word of this meeting reached our offices, with the possibility that I would go to Albany to present our story directly, everyone began to feel a wave of confidence that now we were going to get somewhere. The boss would put this over; that was their attitude. How could he possibly fail?

I too shared in our rather naive certainty that our cause was too just, too necessary, to fail. In retrospect it is easy to see that we were forgetting so many important matters that had to be considered—such things as rules and regulations, accreditation, approval by specific authorities who had to examine every aspect of our proposed school.

But when the appointment was made and Bill Spinelli agreed to go with me to Albany for the conference, none of this was in our minds; nothing was going to stop us now; once the situation was explained to the people up there, the rest would be purely routine.

When I walked out of my office to get into the car with Spinelli, Ellen called after me cockily, "Convince them, boss. We'll be waiting for your word."

I laughed and waved and got into the car.

Bill Spinelli and I drove up there with all our high anticipations and hopes. Bill assured me that Simches was a dedicated human being and that although he might have reservations, once he heard the facts directly, we would have a green light.

When we walked in, however, we were seen not by Simches alone, but also by the head of the Bureau, Dr. Anthony J. Pelone.

The Bureau director obviously was not quite sure of why we were there. Neither Pelone nor Simches had ever met me before nor had they been to Abilities.

I tried to explain the problem. The apparent lack of awareness of how little education those on homebound instruction really received, the need to get these children out of their unnatural isolation, cut off from social contact, other children, people, the world.

The Bureau head informed me that the school districts had a well-worked out program for these children, that they had doctors, psychiatrists, psychologists, every kind of checkup humanly possible, they were getting as much as could be given, as much as they could absorb.

We had our cases—detailed records of twelve children in Nassau County, New York to prove our point. I could demonstrate in each instance how these children could get to our Human Resources building, where, although it was to be an improvised school setup, we did have a special gymnasium for disabled, and a swimming pool. I told them about our camp.

"If they could get to your facility," the Bureau director stated, "they could get to a public school, couldn't they?"

"But there would be stairs to go up and down, there would be the difficulty of handling those who need toileting assistance."

I was reminded that the school districts had never raised these questions. What right did I have to challenge what they had recommended for these children? Mr. Simches suggested that perhaps there was a problem that should be looked into, an inquiry should be made into the whole area, and if what Mr. Viscardi said proved true, then appropriate recommendations should be made.

Dr. Pelone agreed that this might be wise. It was not indicated what kind of action might be followed. The Director then asked Simches to look into the cases of each of the twelve cases from the three school districts and find why they were not going to school and what their individual problems were.

He would have to have those results before him before he could consider the merits of our suggestions.

The meeting was obviously at an end.

Chapter 5

I left this meeting frustrated. I had come to Albany with full confidence in this cause; Ellen was waiting for my call to tell her of our victory, all those who had worked with me were counting on me—and I had failed.

Of course we should have realized all the reasons, all the necessary restrictions and requirements surrounding the starting of a school; of course we were acting on a basis of our closeness to the problem. Here were the children, here we were ready to help. Why, we would have a school by fall!

That was the attitude. To us it was enough that there was a need. In retrospect this was our error; we leapt ahead too fast, we should have recognized the facts, the realities. Bill Spinelli was trying to tell me some of this as we walked out of the building, as he tried to soothe my disappointment.

"Perhaps I should go to the State Capitol right this minute," I said. "To camp on the governor's doorstep until he sees us, to tell him—"

"Hank, even you can't see the governor without an appointment, you know that. These things take time. You can't turn the Department of Education upside down. There are avenues and procedures."

Of course he was right, and I knew it in my heart. It was a bitter moment for me.

I had no idea how warm Simches really might be about this matter. I was upset.

In one of the most important projects I had tried to bring into being, I had failed. There was no other way to interpret what had happened. I was more than disappointed.

The real conflict lay in an area that none of us fully realized: Each of us was looking at the truth as we saw it and knew it to be. School officials who reported to Albany that any child who could go to school was in fact going, were telling the truth. Our certainty that there were children who could go to school but weren't was also true.

The question was: What kind of school? What kind of facilities? What kind of instruction? What were the special needs and how would education have to shift and change and adapt to meet those needs?

We think of ourselves as modern in attitudes and techniques; we forget how close we are to primitive concepts of disability, physical, emotional or mental. Abilities, Inc., was started in order to show the world that the disabled man or woman could do a job in industry—in every area, at every level—that could match his counterpart in the normal world outside.

It was only a few years ago when Abilities began; someone had to start it, to take the lead, to prove this thing in practice, to change attitudes and thinking that should have died out long ago but that persist despite all our advances, all our modernity, all our enlightenment on so many other subjects.

There is still the lingering thought that disability is something evil, the limping foot dragging in the darkness of night, the hunchback in the shadows, the clubfooted one—mankind has endowed these disabilities with an aura of superstition that dies slow and hard.

But where should we begin, really—if not with the youngster who ought to be in school but isn't, with the boy or girl who sits in a lonely room and dreams and dreams of all youth, the big dream of what can be and will be, if only—

If only what?

If only someone else could understand that he or she has a right to his reality as much as any other human being.

This was the low point I think, that ride back from Albany. But I must confess here that this was the point when I was saying to myself, as the car sped over the summer-bright highway, the hell with it. Why should I struggle with this problem? I've got enough to do. I've got Abilities to run, I've got my family, my wife and my four wonderful daughters who hardly see their father. I've got the Human Resources and its research efforts.

It wasn't going to last long, this feeling, this sense of

frustration and total defeat, total futility, but it was there that afternoon on that ride home.

A little later along the Thruway I stopped to call Ellen at Abilities and let her know what had happened. I knew how greatly everybody there was concerned about this meeting.

In a letter written to me from her new home in California, where she has moved with her family, Ellen recalled that phone call:

I can remember certain days in my life most vividly—like the day you first hired me to work for Abilities, and the day the first mass was said in the Abilities interfaith chapel, the day I married Frank, the day my little son was born. And the day you made that journey to Albany for the school and those kids.

I can still see myself waiting and waiting for word, any word. The appointment was early but there was no word and your secretary was so angry with me because I kept bothering her all day long. Then finally the call came through, but you didn't sound like yourself at all. You said, "No, they aren't buying it."

I said, "What do you mean—not buying it?" I must have practically screamed those words into the phone. Everybody started looking at me in the office at Abilities. Then you told me how you'd been told there was no problem and if one did exist they would handle it, not us. There wouldn't be any school. There wouldn't be anything to help these children.

Then I remember you said over the phone, "Ellen, forget it. Why should I be going around like some crazy fool offering our building, our facilities, our firsthand knowledge of disabled children, taking our time and energies from the work of Abilities—for *this*? You said, "Why, Ellen? It's more than I can cope with. I'm just one ordinary guy."

I didn't know what to say. For about the first time in my life,

I was struck dumb. That is, right until you said you were just an ordinary man. No matter how shocked I was, that brought me back to reality.

I remember yelling—actually yelling into the phone—I wonder now why you didn't fire me on the spot for the disrespectful manner in which I spoke to you: "But you're not just one ordinary man—one ordinary man couldn't have lived the life you have led, couldn't have started Abilities, couldn't have borrowed $8,000 and single-handed built it to where it is today. None of that was ordinary. . . ."

You had the long trip back from Albany and I had other work to do but my heart wasn't in it. I didn't even leave with the others at 4:30. I just hung around, talking to Florence. And then you called again—from your home. And this time you sounded like yourself and you didn't say you were just an ordinary man.

But you sure said a lot of things. These children were going to have what they were entitled to—what they deserved. Not operating on archaic methods used for half a century and outmoded and worn out. They were going to have a complete education, and they were going to come out of the kitchens and back rooms and they were going to have *hope*, and they were going to have purposeful lives, and they were going to have love.

Just writing it fills me up so I can barely see my writing for tears in my eyes—and a picture in my mind of myself as a teenager in an apartment five flights up sitting at the kitchen table—waiting for life.

Part II

Homebound Houses

Chapter 6

I called in Dick Switzer and told him, "Dick, I asked you to hold up resigning from the Special Ed department of the Brentwood School District. I'm glad I did. You'd better sign up. We've got problems to solve. We won't be in motion until the fall of 1962."

Delay of at least a year . . . I could see the disappointment on his face yet at the same time I felt the searching in this young educator's expression. Was I quitting on it? Was I really licked for good?"

Did I feel that maybe these children of ours—these children we knew were out there—weren't worth the search, the heartbreak, the beating we were undergoing, to get started?

I wasn't walking out.

And it wasn't because I'm any smarter, more noble, more dedicated, more anything than other people. I had no choice; this responsibility involved too much of my own life, too much of all the lives I have known of, listened to, suffered with and for, in one way or another.

I said to Dick, "We aren't quitting them—or the school

—regardless of what else happens. But there are problems. We've got to work them out."

Problems! We looked at each other and he grinned— this big, awkward-gaited headmaster-to-be, molder of new and imaginative techniques to meet special needs, in a school that was as yet only a barren blueprint in our minds.

And might never be anything more.

It is almost always when we feel close to the edge, close to thinking the world has walked out on us—that we find we are wrong; the help is there, we have to know it is there.

Two seemingly unrelated events occurred within days of my return from the disaster at Albany. Each played an important part in the future of the school.

The first was an impromptu visit to Abilities by Ray Simches.

He had said that he was coming but I had not anticipated it would be that soon after the Albany meeting. The assistant to Dr. Pelone in the Bureau for Handicapped Children wanted to see for himself. A tall, thoughtful academically-oriented public official.

He paid us a call—and told me a story.

I walked with him through our buildings on that visit. He was startled at our modern, gleaming structure, set amid gardens and beauty, all on one floor so that one had to roll wheelchairs uphill; he saw men in wheelchairs, legs paralyzed, men and women at workbenches with every assorted disability known to the medical profession; he saw one of our estimating experts, paralyzed from the waist down from a shellburst, carrying on his job on a full-length litter. He saw Alex running around the plant overseeing packaging problems and other highly technical details—Alex who can open a package of sugar and pour it into his coffee without spilling a grain—legless, armless, handless.

He saw not a hospital, not a backroom refuge for the despaired-of and despairing, not a place for *cripples*—he saw human beings, laughing, talking, working, producing, earning, living. He saw a sense of dignity and purpose in lives which would otherwise be meaningless.

He came into the Human Resources building and watched the camp program. He saw the children swimming in the pool.

Afterwards, he told me: "I had to see this. There are so many who try to do things like this—but this is so very different. This has meaning."

I came to understand how deeply these children concerned him, what he had seen here, the relationship in vocational terms with the adults he had witnessed at work in Abilities itself.

In the course of this conversation he said, "In terms of your philosophy of life, you must have had some moment when you said to yourself, what's the purpose of all this, how best can I devote my energy, my intelligence, my interest—and you decided to develop it and direct it toward other disabled persons."

I was thinking back to the moment when Bernard Baruch and Dr. Rusk had asked me to come into this work
for the disabled.

He seemed to know or guess my answer. "I had a similar experience," he said. "Maybe as a result of the war,
seeing so many human lives wasted. Tanks and guns
weren't expendable—human beings were. Somehow I decided—right after the war—that whatever time I had left I
was not going to sell cars or food—I'd been a salesman. If
I was going to sell anything it would be values—for people. So—I shifted my work, gradually, into education, into
the field of people, of people I could help."

Simches paused a moment, then went on, "So perhaps
now you can understand my reaction to seeing your organization, these men and women at work, those children
laughing, shouting, swimming in that pool."

A little further along in our talk he mentioned a young
disabled person in whose case he was interested—a young
woman with a spastic condition who was having great difficulty getting work. "Is there . . . is this the kind of person
you could use here?"

I told him quite possibly it was. There were many cut-
backs in contracts at that time but in the summer season
there was always vacation time and need for temporary
replacements. "Give me her name, tell her to apply."

I didn't think much about this casual suggestion. The
young lady did apply and did work for us during the later
part of the summer.

Months afterwards, when Ray and I had become good

friends, he was to relate to me the full meaning of this young woman and her role in our own story.

"It was in thinking of Kathy, remembering her, that I caught the real need for the kind of school you were talking about," Ray explained. "She had this spastic condition and was on home instruction throughout childhood and early adolescence.

"I've known her since she was about twelve. I got to know her not as a person with a disability, but as someone who dreamed as people dream, hoped as people hope, suffered the frustrations people suffer.

"When she was on home instruction, everything she was led to believe was that once she got her high school diploma and finished home teaching, all the doors would be open. This was what they said, what she believed.

"She finished her education on home instruction. She reported to school in the auditorium, was given her diploma with the graduating class and much to-do was made about her. And three months after her graduation—Kathy was a forgotten girl.

"That's when I asked what Abilities might have open for her, even for a few weeks or months . . ."

That was the way Ray Simches really was, the way he felt and thought as a man and as an official.

The second unusual event that proved the world hadn't quite walked out on us or the children was a phone call I received from a lawyer, a distinguished white-haired gentleman of unimpeachable standing in our community.

I knew him only by his distinguished reputation. He introduced himself over the phone, apologized for bothering me, stated that he was anxious to have a meeting with me to discuss a matter of great urgency and importance— my plan to start a school for handicapped children.

"I am an old man with arthritis," he said. "I want to see you. My home is half a mile from yours—on the Sound. Can you come here tonight?"

I could—and did.

We sat together on the terrace of his house, looking out on the gleaming lights of the Bronx Whitestone Bridge. He had rumpled white hair, furrowed skin, hard lines of battle on his face. He had the somewhat brusque manner of the courthouse trial attorney. "I'm taking it upon myself to give you some advice," he began abruptly.

"Why?"

"Because my suggestion will solve your problem."

"Who told you about our plan to start a school—who brought it to your attention?"

"Let me tell you something," he said completely ignoring my question. "The Department of Education, even if they want to, can't help. It's too long. Too much red tape. You and your great idea for those children will wither on the vine waiting—if you try that way."

"You're suggesting I give up this idea, abandon it and the children?"

"I'm suggesting you try another tack. Did you ever hear," he asked, "of the Vocational Education and Extension Board of Nassau County?"

I looked at him questioningly. "As a start," he said, "your school could be launched under the administration of this Board. They have a budget for this kind of thing, this special group sort of thing. Technically they would be in charge. They would hire your facilities for the school. You may never have heard of this Board but—"

I did know about it, actually. It was an educational agency run by the county, founded many years past for the training of firemen and fire departments in local communities. Gradually other unusual groups had come under its control and general supervision—the training and education of brain-damaged and retarded children, for example.

The old lawyer smiled, sitting there in the dusk, puffing on a cigar that glowed red in the shadows.

His point was clear. It was a way to begin. It was an end run around red tape and the slow evolution of entrenched tradition.

I thanked him. I promised him that his suggestion would have my earnest and deepest and immediate consideration.

I had—and still have—no idea who brought the school matter to his attention. I know that when I spoke of this idea to others working with me the immediate reaction was favorable. Both Campbell and Spinelli voted yes on the idea.

I learned that Ray Simches was carrying an extremely heavy work load at that particular juncture; since our first meeting the Bureau for Handicapped Children had been divided into two separate but equal bureaus, one handling the mentally retarded children, under the direction of Dr. Pelone, the other for the physically disabled, the latter under the direct control of Ray Simches.

This development also, I felt, could have vast importance on the destiny of our school.

Ray approved the idea. He approved the idea of marrying private facilities to the Vocational Board's control—and budgetary backing. It had been done in other communities. Theoretically we would provide the facilities for a school for seriously crippled children on home instruction. In actuality, we would provide far more—staff, techniques, operational control and development. It would be done in cooperation with the school districts—they might oppose outsiders seeking data but they were accustomed to cooperating with the Vocational Board.

Simches told me, "You've hit on the one avenue, in my opinion, that will work, if there is a need for the program and if it will be supported by the school districts."

So in the late fall of 1961 the slightly sidetracked dream of the school was back on the road.

In a letter I had written to Mary Switzer, Dick's aunt, the day after my return from Albany, I told her that if I had failed in Albany, it was only temporarily.

"Now I have some real incentives," I wrote, "to overcome the obstacles, gather more knowledge, and find a way for us to begin the program either in February or in a year from September."

The new target date for the school, if further obstacles

did not loom up, or further doors slam shut, was September 1962.

A small mountain of spade work had to be done first. The plan was that the Human Resources Foundation would lease facilities technically, swimming pool, classrooms, recreational rooms, to the Vocational Board. In practice, the school would be staffed, directed and operated by us.

We arranged the first meeting with the Vocational Board. We had several preliminary discussions and discovered that important educational officials of the county thoroughly approved of our plan for the severely crippled child; it fitted in well with the Board's general program.

The first two steps, we agreed, would be formation of a committee to seek closer cooperation of all school districts in the county—cooperation which we had not had in first efforts in this area. Our second step would be to make a careful survey to establish beyond any doubt the extent of the need, the available students, their present status, the problems of transportation and similar technical details.

This committee, of which I was a member, included leaders of the several school districts, Fred Shore from East Meadow, Marvin Gibson and Bill Campbell from Hicksville, Ray Simches, Dr. Jean Schultz, of the Nassau County health department, Virginia Keller of Levittown, and others of similar posts and knowledge in the field. The committee's prime purpose was to ride herd on the program, to make sure it developed in an orderly, practical and responsible way with regard to the interests of all parties concerned—community, county, state, staff, educational standards—and the children themselves.

We decided on a second step, to find someone who would get facts for use. I went to my friend David Heyman of the New York Foundation and told him of our pressing need for money to hire an investigator to ferret out a flock of hidden children. Ellen at that time had moved with her husband and family to California, and Bill Campbell by then was tied down by his duties with the Hicksville school district. Dave Heyman is quick to appreciate new ideas and his foundation gave us a planning grant. Now we could really comb the area to find these children.

The young lady I brought in to fill this presumably temporary post was to become far more important in this blueprint for a school than I could have guessed at that time.

Her name was Bobbi Housman, nee Roberta Yanover. She was a registered nurse and Adelphi College graduate and she was the daughter of the doctor who years before had taken me to a legmaker on Third Avenue to get my first set of artificial limbs.

She was also the dark-haired, blue-eyed bride of the distinguished young American painter, Russ Housman. They had just returned East from the Midwest where Russ had been painting and teaching art at a university.

I tried to give Bobbi some idea of what this assignment would mean. I explained that it would be far more than merely collecting names or data; that would be only a first step. "You've got to get into those homes, see the parents and the doctors, talk with them, meet these children. You'll find doors slammed in your face . . ."

A remarkably controlled young woman, not unlike her father in the depth of emotion that does not show on the surface, Bobbi agreed to start at once on this difficult quest.

The Vocational Board agreed to send out a letter to school districts informing them about her mission and asking them to give any help or information she would require.

I brought in Frank Gentile from Abilities as over-all administrator of the new Human Resources School, with Dick Switzer as future headmaster. A polio victim, Frank can ambulate with braces but is usually in his chair.

Our staff was beginning to take its first definitive shape. We were a school in the process of being born. Each individual had his job to do. Our arrangements with the Vocational Board had to be evolved; who took orders from whom and on what basis. Teachers had to be found, staff who could handle children lacking any experience in education outside the home; techniques had to be discussed, evolved, educational processes considered, explored and crystallized.

Every question opened the doors to dozens of others.

Through the fall and winter and into the spring and summer of 1962, the tension was to grow month by month as Bobbi's work with the children and the school districts continued and the program and the school came closer to a day of actual beginning.

In the course of that period of formation, we owed our existence to many people, of different ideas and motives. None, I think, had any more important a part to play in that time, despite his hands-off attitude officially, than Ray Simches.

One letter I prize deeply came to me from Ray Simches after that first time he came to see us at Abilities.

"During my recent visit," he wrote, "we discussed many . . . problems in the field of programs for handicapped children. However, I would be remiss if I did not react to both Abilities, Inc., and Human Resources, on a purely personal level.

"The past 20 years have given rise to Buchenwald and Dachau whose prime purpose was the resolution of a problem by murder, degradation and inhumanity. It is nice to know that during this period of time there was the development of Abilities, Inc., which stressed life, respect and integrity. For the Eichmann's of the world it is nice to know there are the Viscardi's . . ."

Chapter 7

One night in late fall, 1962, shortly after she came to work in the newly organized but not yet operating Human Resources School, Bobbi Housman had a date to meet a child—and its parents.

She set out on this assignment, as she was to do many more times, with hardly any idea at all of what she would find. Each situation was the same and each different. Each home, each family, each child. Each one is its own story with its special need, its special challenge, and its special promise.

Tonight it was a little girl. The school district official who provided the name was able to tell Bobbi only, "The child is fifteen, they say, very bright, but also very severely handicapped. Has no mobility whatsoever. They haven't tried to teach her to read . . ."

When Bobbi had first been handed this assignment, she and Frank Gentile had sat together at a desk before a blank piece of paper. It had to be a fresh start. The names Ellen and Bill had compiled earlier in the year would not do; we had been thinking at that time of older adolescents;

now we were thinking in terms of younger children too, down to the elementary and primary levels.

In addition, lists like this quickly become outdated; people move, parents are seeking some place to go with their child. Some children had been handed their homebound diplomas. They were officially "graduated."

The letter sent out by the Vocational Board to the school districts stated in part, "There has been an interest expressed at both local and state levels in setting up a special educational program for children who up till now have been homebound. These physically handicapped children have been homebound because of the lack of available special transportation, special school buildings, and/or special physical education classes.

"These children are long term, 'permanent' physically handicapped, not the typically short term fractures or medical cases for whom home tutoring is provided.

"Before any further planning of a complex nature can be undertaken, it is necessary to know the numbers and types of such youngsters . . .

"Since such a service as is being contemplated could only be made available on a cooperative basis, several school districts have approached the state and the Vocational Education and Extension Board for help in this matter.

"We are asking your cooperation . . ."

This letter drew a number of responses and Bobbi set out first to visit those districts that seemed most anxious to cooperate, ready to provide information, detailed data, names and addresses.

She was discouraged by the gap in understanding that existed, even now, even with these districts and officials who were most eager to cooperate. She found that many of them simply did not understand what we were driving at, talking about, so meagre was the general knowledge of what the homebound children really were like, their problems and needs.

Reporting on one day's activity, Bobbi told me, "These children they are writing to us about so far are all suffering from a temporary disability or illness, despite the letter. A fractured leg, a broken collarbone or something like that. When I simply have to tell them the whole story of what we want they find it so hard to believe. They seem almost shocked at the kind of children we're interested in, when I tell them."

But Bobbi kept at her job, beginning by visiting all of these school districts, talking to school officials in each one, gradually making them understand, gradually locating the people who worked with homebound children in that area, gradually compiling the names and addresses of the hidden half-children behind their closed suburban doors.

One school superintendent told her blandly that so far as he knew there were no such children in his district at all. But he did suggest that Mrs. Housman speak with one teacher in the school. "She's quite interested in that sort of thing . . ."

Bobbi did speak with this teacher and the woman provided her instantly with the name and address of another homebound child in that district, a difficult disability case, a little girl of eight years old.

Bobbi explained, "This is the kind of child that gets really forgotten because it doesn't fit in with anything."

With all the good will in the world, these educators are simply overworked running the job they have to do for normal kids. And with the not-so-normal, like this spina bifida eight-year-old, they say, "How can anyone find the time and what could we do for her?"

This was why the school had to be—to teach children like these to live within the fullness of limitations and lack of limitations, to prepare them for what they will have to meet and deal with—and to help them to learn how.

And this is why Bobbi went out into the byways of the communities, over back streets and down bleak paths, as well as into some of the finest homes and neighborhoods, knocking on closed doors. Once we were to become known the children would come forth. But it is amazing to recall how reluctant parents, doctors and schools were in providing the names of these children.

Many parents were, at first, suspicious, dubious, questioning and uncooperative. Too many of them had been fooled before by people calling with plans and ideas that proved to be wild schemes and promotions designed to milk the children, not to meet their need but to feed upon it.

Many parents thought that Bobbi was trying to sell them an encyclopedia or was a social worker on an investigation. They had lived so long with their own insecurity, their own hopes for their child, and wondering how these might be fulfilled and seeing no chance of it, that they dared not accept a stranger at the door.

On all of these possible students for the school whose names and background Bobbi Housman obtained from the school districts, she compiled full information, everything available before making preliminary contact with the parents.

Yet the game of secrecy ran on. One woman residing in an expensive housing development put on a performance of great shock. "Handicapped child? There is no handicapped child in this home."

Before her, as she was calling, Bobbi had the full report on the woman's son; the boy was seriously malformed, could not ambulate and was incontinent. He had never been to school, had always had a private tutor and never left the house.

Bobbi tried to explain the new program, the new school, the possibility that it might be of particular value to this woman and her son, the benefits of having a child in the schoolroom with other children.

"My son!" the woman echoed. "Let me explain to you —my son is not in any way disabled. My son is a genius. We're having him tutored . . . We are sending him to Harvard. He is going to Harvard College . . ."

And she hung up.

It was a world of suspicion, disbelief, defenses thrown up against hurt, against assault, against further rejection.

"You represent some social agency, don't you? You want to take the child from us. But you can't. We won't let you. We'll fight it . . ."

"I'm not from an agency, I'm not trying to take your child . . ."

Sometimes she would telephone, sometimes the people had no phone, no way of being reached without a personal visit. Often they thought it was some kind of sales pitch when she telephoned. "What are you trying to sell us? Whatever it is, we don't want it."

And the click of the phone.

Yet it would be unfair to say they were all like this. Bobbi did find many cooperative parents, doctors and school people. They were not all difficult. Some were most grateful and eager to hear more about the School.

One of the more moving experiences was a visit Bobbi made alone one night in the late fall to the home of a bright fifteen-year-old girl.

A pleasant, simple, white framed house. It set back from the street and there was a white picket fence in front. Like other homebound houses it has a certain withdrawn air; a charm, a garden out front, yet somehow the feeling of isolation, the protective wall.

Tonight there were lights in the window. Bobbi had talked with the mother on the phone and made the appointment.

A man and woman answered her ring at that front door. They were well-dressed, smiling, gracious; typical suburbanites, one might have thought, typical suburban parents.

The woman was dark-haired in a plain dark dress, the man in a business suit.

The whole house had an immaculate air. They had evidently gone to much effort to make everything right, everything perfect, for this visitation.

Yet they still had a residue of suspicion in words and tone, even as they greeted her.

The mother asked: "You say you're with the Nassau County Vocational Board—something about our little girl, something about a school?"

"I told you on the phone, you remember," Bobbi said. "It's about a school we're starting, the Human Resources School . . ."

They did not quite understand. What was this new school? They had heard of Hank Viscardi. They had heard about a place called Abilities. What did all that have to do with them or their daughter?

The father told Bobbi bluntly, "As far as any school goes—how could our Dotty ever go to any school, anywhere? How?"

The woman put a hand on her husband's, "You said you'd at least listen. We ought to do that much."

"All right, I'll listen," he told Bobbi.

He explained that the doctors had told them there was nothing they could do, nothing anyone could do for their little girl. "That's how she is, the way she'll always have to be."

This man and woman led Bobbi from the foyer into their nicely furnished living room. There was an upright piano in one corner, a large sofa and overstuffed chairs, the reproduction of a religious painting on one wall. On the table Bobbi observed a portrait photograph—the face of a lovely child, a girl with light golden hair and dark eyes.

The mother said, "That's Dorothea."

"Lovely little girl. Is she here?"

"Upstairs."

"Does she—do you bring her downstairs often?"

The mother said, "No, we don't bring her down. Practically never. It's too difficult for us and for her. We're afraid. We might hurt her. We could trip on the stairs. We could . . ."

The father explained to Bobbi. "She's as happy up there. Bringing her down—it doesn't mean anything. Where can she go anyway—what can she do?"

"Do people come to see her? Children, other children on the block, in the neighborhood?"

The parents shook their heads. "A teacher comes from the school district once or twice a week," the mother explained. "Reads to her, tells her about history. Dotty doesn't ask any more if she can go to school. She knows."

"But perhaps it would be the best thing in the world for her, if she could," Bobbi told them.

Bobbi felt that the father seemed disturbed at her insistence on this as a possibility. It was as if this were something they would like to believe but did not dare.

"Could I see your daughter?"

The mother said, "Of course you can see Dotty. Come."

They went with her up the stairs to the second floor; into a room furnished with gay nursery wall paper and lacy frilly curtains at the windows. Lamplight filled this room with a rose-warm glow. The parents explained that the windows faced out on the backyard; there were trees and a view of a wooded residential area beyond.

This was Dotty's world, this room, these windows and their view.

A portion of Bobbi Housman's report on this child reads as follows:

"I was impressed with Dotty and what we might do for her. She presents an unusual problem.

"Dorothea was in a very pretty nightgown and her hair, which is light, was fixed very prettily. She has very little movement of her body but she smiled and greeted me with obvious warmth and high interest. She has a very pretty smile. One hand is paralyzed, the other partially. She has no movement or sensation in either leg.

"Despite the serious paralysis, which dates back to when she was three years old, and despite numerous stays in various hospitals, she has a very happy and gay nature. Because of the number of hospitalizations in the past, plus the moves the family made in efforts to find the best environment for her, her education has been spasmodic and wholly inadequate by any definition.

"Her home teacher does help her, in her mother's opinion. The mother says the teacher spends a great deal of time talking about her world, her activities in summer sports, winter skiing and such things. Learning to read, write, spell or study history, comes slowly, very slowly. The teacher says, "We're really not ready for that yet." This seems to be the attitude.

"The girl is very interested in music and likes to listen to the record player; this is her main outlet.

"I spent some time with Dorothea and her parents. I explained what our school was, how it would function, how transportation would be worked out with the local school districts, that we would not know what class she would fit into until we were able to test her, and we would have to consider all factors before we could be sure she could come but I personally was in favor of it.

"As they listened, their whole manner changed, as both parents realized what this could mean to their daughter— she happens to be their only child. From the almost antagonistic attitude the father had displayed when I first arrived, he was full of ideas and suggestions on his own, for carrying Dorothea up and down the stairs at home, in the morning when she left, or the afternoon coming home.

"I said I would like them to see Abilities and the Human Resources building where the school will be housed and the swimming pool, the gym and the bowling alleys. It was agreed that Dorothea would come on this visit also. The child was overjoyed at this prospect of seeing the Human Resources building and the possibility of attending school there. She kept asking me, "Do you think they will take me? Is there really a chance they will take me in your school?" ·

"I left her with the assurance that we would all do everything we could—we, the school staff and her own parents, to make this come true for her."

Dotty's was one random case out of a small-sized army.

Not all could be accepted, not all wanted to come. Many parents had fears and reservations and held back. This was, after all, an experimental school and neither Bobbi nor her aides in this preliminary work made any efforts to conceal that fact.

We were a school unlike any other school, dealing with students most of whom were never before in regular classes.

A boy of sixteen with a reading and writing level of ten. A good looking, handsome lad but he must ride in a wheelchair. There is trouble in the home, too, because the father does not want to accept this boy. He does not want a crippled son.

But Bobbi meets them, Bobbi talks to them, particularly to the mother and boy . . . he will come to school.

The problem will be worked on, the changing of the attitude of the father.

Here is a chubby little girl on a litter, she has a serious disability but she will improve, the doctors report. She is ten.

Bobbi's recommendation: "Parents cooperative and understanding. This child desperately needs social contacts however . . ."

Here are two children, brother and sister, with a blood condition that requires them to have transfusions every four or five weeks. Their bodies are small, they dress them like children of eight or nine; but they are fifteen years old. They become difficult, the mother tells Bobbi, when the time comes for them to have their transfusions. They said to me, please, Mummy, we have to get our new blood. . . ."

Parents in these cases are torn by ambivalent feelings. They are interested, hopeful, anxious and frightened. They want to be sure about the medical care, about their own doctors, about what they can expect for their children at the school.

Some of the parents actually have no family doctors; some of the children Bobbi saw were wearing wornout braces, braces that didn't fit; many of them were in serious need of medical care.

Bobbi explained all the services the school would provide, the medical care, the investigation, the physical therapist and special studies that would be provided for each child; the programming that would be conducted so that school districts would provide special buses to carry the child to the Human Resources School.

Bobbi, Dick and our staff interviewed more than two hundred parents, either by phone or personal visits.

Generally, most of the parents were delighted to hear of our program because they were so dissatisfied with the methods and results of homebound tutoring. They were aware that the child was being deprived both of rounded education and of social contacts normal in childhood.

The medical aspects and the special care they felt their child required were the two main issues. Most of their questions were answered when they visited Abilities and

Human Resources, saw the medical department maintained along with the research staff, the facilities available at Human Resources, the lifeguard protection in the pool, the care in organization because all of us at Abilities have a greater safety consciousness than the average level in normal society.

To the children themselves, the meaning of this new school had far greater impact than even these parents could grasp in some instances.

For them it was liberation, a beginning of reality beyond the protective walls the parents had built. For despite the love that went into that protection the child still must find himself and his world on his own.

From earliest awareness the child wonders about school —where will he start? Others in the family and the neighborhood have begun. When will he go? For these children the question becomes: Will I go? Will any school take me? Will I be able to get there?

Gradually the awareness dawns on the homebound— the answer is no. Not for them.

"It's like you think of something for a long time, you think there must be something and you don't know what it is," one fourteen-year-old boy told Bobbi. "And then— there it is. There is the school."

For each child it is different, individual, yet for each it is the same—the incredible promise that is almost a reality. For Dotty as for the others.

Her mother informed us that she could hardly wait for our report. At least half a dozen times in the week to ten days following their visit to our grounds, her mother called to ask Bobbi, "Is there any news about when she can come or not?"

But a school is a school. It must have its procedures and its standards and it must maintain them at the highest possible level for all students in order to be of value to any. We had to know that Dorothea could fit into this program. All the figures and facts added up the answer we finally had to give: Dorothea received her letter telling her that she was accepted.

We could not tell her what class—what subjects—none of the other details. Her mother called us and told us, "Dotty can't wait until fall—she's so excited and thrilled. She keeps telling us, "Mommy, isn't it wonderful? I'm going to go to school—like other children.""

Chapter 8

||||||||||||||||||||||||||||||||||||||||||||||||||||||||||||||||||||

Gradually word of our school got around. Out of the bushes of suburbia, the lonely houses and backrooms, they came to us, some hearing of us and calling, others after we had located and found them; they came on crutches and canes, in wheelchairs and on litters; fat and thin, short and tall, legless, armless, diabetic, with heart conditions and muscle disabilities; with all the assorted deformities—but also with their eyes full of tomorrow, their tomorrow.

Bobbi visited personally more than forty homes, in addition to the scores of phone calls. The most probable children, those who stood to gain most from such a school, had to be called out.

We had planned only twelve to fourteen in all for the first year; we wound up with twenty-one enrolled, and a waiting list.

Many parents, Bobbi discovered, decided their child would be better off on home tutoring rather than risking this new school. Doctors were conservative and concerned on other cases. Many parents did not have the personal courage to let go, to let their child out of their immediate personal control.

Some of the stories of this period of development, with the staff building on one side and the public, the programs, the planning on the other, have already become legends of hope and despair, victory and loss, in the story of the school.

It was a time of action in many various directions; all of the kettles boiling and bubbling in that time of preparation. Each step important, each development, each new child.

One of the children was a girl with a condition that made it difficult for her to walk, produced awkward distortions and spastic motions in the face and body. The medical name of this condition is *dystonia musculorum deformans*. It is congenital in origin, and leads to progressive loss of muscular or neurologic function. It is characterized by a peculiar twisting spasm of the muscles.

She had had several operations, none of which had corrected the basic condition. The condition was, however, stabilized; it was not progressive. The mother put her into public school. The principal of the school kept calling the girl down out of the classroom for one reason or another; he admitted to the mother that he simply could not tolerate this girl in school; he could not look at her, yet he could not stay away from her. He would call the teacher on the phone every twenty minutes to find out how she was getting along, "What's happening with Mae?"

The mother went to the superintendent of schools and

told her what was happening. "My girl is doing all her work well. She's capable of taking care of herself. Her condition is stabilized; it is not getting worse. Why does the principal badger her like this, badger us?"

The superintendent said only, "Well, he is very likely afraid you or your husband might bring a lawsuit against us if something went wrong."

"Is there any reason she shouldn't go to school?"

"No, not in any legal or educational sense. But, of course, the principal, it is his school, he's in charge and if he doesn't want her he doesn't have to accept her. These are difficult matters to understand."

"Well, all he is doing is torturing her, himself and us," the mother stated flatly. "I think he is very troubled. He doesn't want her there and he doesn't want to let her go."

This mother had heard—through friends—about Human Resources and its proposed school. She spoke to her husband about this possibility but his answer was, "How do we know—it could be good or bad. Can we take a chance?"

"We could find out."

One Sunday, the mother suggested, "Why don't we go over there to Human Resources—maybe it will be open."

So that afternoon, the parents and the girl drove to the grounds. There was no one around; all the doors were locked. But one shade was up in the main auditorium of the Human Resources Building and they were able to peek inside.

To the girl, a glimpse like this was a promise. Her mind

read all the details of which she had heard but could not see. Classrooms, gym, swimming pool. Other youngsters. She told her parents, "Look—I—I'll do anything you want if you can get me into this school."

They told her, "Somehow—we'll do it."

They did.

Bobbi's original assignment had been to determine on the basis of a solid survey, with the full cooperation this time of the school district officers, the fact that there was a considerable number of such children as we described— severely, permanently physically disabled boys and girls who could not go to schools because the schools were not equipped to handle such extreme disabilities. This we had now determined beyond any question.

The whole purpose of our school, as I and my associ- ates envisioned it, was to be an incentive for living; a school where the isolated child would be isolated no longer, where the social, recreational, educational compe- tition, the give and take of life, would be available as a part of natural, everyday living; participation in the normal world, to the fullest measure possible, would be- come the accepted norm—including the attitudes of the public, even the staring, the thoughtless remark, all of it faced squarely, understood—this was the educational ob- jective of our proposed Human Resources School. Reha- bilitation and medical care were secondary objectives.

The types of disabilities in these children coming to us involved all forms. They were spelled out in long medical terminology all of which had added up previously to a single phrase full of emptiness and bitter frustration: *homebound* child.

Yet in our minds none of these were cases at all—they were children, boys and girls ranging in age from four or five to sixteen or seventeen. Each a life, each a story, a challenge; each came to us in his own special way.

School officials who were genuinely concerned, visitors to Abilities, private and public health agencies all knew of the proposed school; someone would hear of a child and soon a call would come to Mrs. Housman's desk, "I wonder if you would be interested in this boy in Garden City who had only one leg and one arm but who—"

The stream of the unwanted, the strange array of the hidden children, continued to come. Their parents, their loved ones came.

While all of this was going on, through the late fall of 1961 and the winter and spring of 1962, we were at the same time carrying on an array of additional activities in association with our plans for the school. These were not haphazard plans, they were long-range concepts to which we were committing ourselves and our energies.

Hiring the faculty was one of the big jobs that continued concurrently. Dick Switzer recognized all the pitfalls in this area, yet he was concerned with one objective; to get the best faculty possible, the best teaching, in terms of the demands and requirements for understanding, drive, ambition, need, functional teaching talents and techniques, that this school needed.

Our first faculty consisted of Alice Clingan, a school nurse, teacher, and Dick Switzer, in a single classroom.

Ironically—or perhaps fittingly—among the first teachers we accepted was a home education teacher who had learned of the school and applied to us; since the Nassau County Vocational Board was technically and officially running the show, and only hiring our facilities on a rental basis, all teachers had to be hired actually by the Board. Instructions to us were: "If you find good ones, send them over with your recommendations, and we'll hire them."

Our former home teacher, Mrs. Sally Fitch, was one of the first additions to the staff, after Dick, Bobbi and Frank Gentile. From her record we know that she was an extraordinarily conscientious teacher. We had reports that she had spent extra hours with individual homebound students, to bring them up to the level of their age and ability. In home teaching, she was an outstanding example of dedicated effort.

This effort she has given to the school—almost from the first day she was hired. She had, of course, dealt with many grades and levels in her home teaching work; now she had to learn the specific requirements for the seventh, eighth and ninth grade junior-high level she would be starting.

From the moment she was actually hired, in the early summer of 1962, this dark-haired young woman devoted herself exclusively, under Dick's direction and suggestion, to developing the curriculum for these classes; she was in contact by mail or telephone with officials in Albany, to make sure that her level of instruction would be as high or higher than required by New York State regents.

One of the subjects required in junior-high seventh-grade level was New York State history. Because of this, she spent weeks of that summer flying around New York State in a Piper Cub plane, taking pictures of historic sites, moments of importance in the country's development, Revolutionary scenes in New York, along the Hudson, Ticonderoga and Saratoga, farmland beside the quiet river just above Saratoga, where the tide of the whole war was changed.

It was her idea that these pictures, particularly for children who had been kept so long immobile by their disabilities, would provide them with a scope of interest and understanding wider than might be obtained in a usual technique or textbook—these pictures taken from the skies.

We hired another teacher after Mrs. Fitch—Mrs. Frances Silverblank who came to us in the spring also, a fully accredited teacher both by New York City and New York State. She had been working at a school for gifted children. She wanted a job with us. We told her we couldn't afford to pay very much.

She said, "I don't care what I'm paid. I want to teach and work with these children you're planning to bring in here."

"You want to be a volunteer?"

"Not at all. I want to be staff, professional staff."

She went to work on a basis of teaching in the English department and the Remedial Reading department—one of the most vital because many of our children are extremely weak in reading skills.

Another brilliant, imaginative teacher brought in that first year was suggested to us by Bobbi Housman's husband, Russ. Russ was teaching art in the Mineola school district and spotted the science teacher there, Sam Nemarich.

Nemarich was interested but hesitant. He loved to teach, he loved the challenge of teaching. But he had never before worked with disabled children. "I don't know how to teach them. I wouldn't want to cheat them out of learning someone else could give them better than I could. Don't you need special training for this sort of thing?"

Dick Switzer explained that this could be provided. Special training could be helpful but was not the whole answer or even a major part.

"I don't want just a Special Ed teacher," Dick told the science man. "I want a good teacher. I don't care what the background is as long as he knows his subject and knows how to teach. If you know how to teach—you can teach the disabled."

Nemarich was the next appointee on the staff. He was to develop a whole new avenue for teaching science to the disabled.

And so the plans went forward, the tempo increased—and the tension.

We had planned for twelve pupils and actually had twenty-one. The Vocational Board had to set its budgets and its payment plans—each school district paid for each child they sent to our school. Bobbi and others on the staff had to make home visits checking to make sure each child selected met the criteria we had established: They had to be permanently physically disabled and of at least average intelligence, so that they would be able to benefit from the school experience.

We checked with family doctors to seek their advice about the child—in a number of cases we found there was no family doctor; we brought in our own pediatrician, one of the greatest in this field, Dr. Leon Greenspan, head of pediatrics at Dr. Rusk's Institute of Physical Medicine and Rehabilitation. Leon Greenspan was an old friend whom I had known in my work with Dr. Rusk. In addition to his Boards in Pediatrics, he was accredited in Physical Medicine and Rehabilitation. He loved children and he believed in what we wanted to do. In those early days we used Vocational Board psychologists to guide in our tests of the youngsters. These were preliminary; later we had our own tests for the children. That part was in the future; at the beginning no one could have told precisely in what grade a child might fit; children deprived of any education cannot be measured by standard age equivalents.

Transportation loomed as a major issue. At first we thought that we would use our special bus with a hydraulic lift so that the children could be lifted on their wheelchairs right into the bus. Then we learned that the school districts would cooperate with us on transportation if we could give their pupil personnel officials some guidance in handling of disabled children. It had been recommended that we put a matron on each bus but we decided it would be better for the children not to have any special overseers; with proper precautions and understanding matrons would be unnecessary.

We told the bus company about the new small carryall wagons that could be purchased. Ramps could inexpensively and easily be fashioned of aluminum or plywood. Wheelchairs could be boarded. We warned them against lifting the child; the less the child is lifted or has to be aided, the better and the safer. Disability has to be limited; it should not be all-encompassing. The child should start to learn to do things independently, there should be minimum assistance, lifting and carrying is not one of the minimums. We knew there would be exceptions. Also we learned school bus drivers have warm hearts.

We developed the curriculum, we brought in additional staff, Russ Housman for art and Elinor DeMott for music —we discovered these areas greatly lacking in homebound children's training. We also had a physical therapist from the Nassau County public health office, Letitia Carney. We found a French teacher and we brought in a trained librarian, Ruth Velleman. The school curriculum had to be full and round. We wanted our children to become future leaders and future teachers; we wanted to give them as much content as possible with every aspect of the regular school training.

The real problem we had to face was of another kind— techniques and methods. This was where we had to adapt and fit program and pupil. How do you have a quadra-plegic hand in an essay? Do you let them give it verbally? But they can't give it verbally all the time. So we have to begin to think of a concept of how they are going to write. Do you just let them make big scrawls with a big crayon that they hold in whatever they have left of arms or hands?

We followed two basic principles: One was that you—everybody—has to learn how to adapt to the world, to make use of whatever ability you have to the best and fullest degree. The other was that we didn't want this school to be different, that is, so different that students would never be in contact with the hard facts of reality. Each must be taught and encouraged to develop compen-sating qualities to offset the extremes of physical makeup, to learn to live fully with what he has left.

Our stress was on academics and there was no right to lie down on the job just because of a wheelchair. We would do everything for a student to get him up to a good working level but we wouldn't feel sorry for him and give him an A in English merely because he can't walk. He gets the A if he tried and succeeds to the best of his ability.

We did find, for example, that electric typewriters are a great help. The keys work very easily and most of our children, however badly disabled, are able to use them, and to learn to write with them. Compensating qualities offset the extremes of physical disability. Adaptation is a trifold problem: what you have to work with, what you have or can devise to work with in life—a typewriter, a workbench, a way of holding a book with one arm and hand—whatever it may be, you use that; the third element is the experienced teacher, working to help this disabled child learn to adapt, to use, to live.

We went over dozens of items that had to be planned for, considered, debated, evolved: a large one-room classroom was fashioned from several rooms in our recreation area. Where would the children come in—through which entrance? Where would they hang up their coats and hats —how high should the coat racks be so that the children could hang up their things independently? Where and how would they carry their books—would there be book shelves underneath the desk? [No, because the wheelchair interferes.] We went through all of these details in our planning. Where would they have lunch? We decided this one simply. Our friends and neighbors in the Herricks School District would provide the food, which the children would eat at special tables but in the main Abilities cafeteria.

A school set in the woods for handicapped youngsters was not my objective. A school here at Abilities, where each day they could see several hundred disabled people at work in all levels of an industrial and artistic operation— from designing glass to wiring airplane wings and data processing—from executive to newest line worker—this family of the disabled could give them a whole new concept.

This was a going world of work, a day's work for a day's pay, and here they could see that they were not limited to doing some kind of made-work activity in some attic workshop; here they could mingle with a world in action, a world that held out to them a promise of how far they might go, each in his own way.

During this somewhat turbulent period we became increasingly aware of an additional problem; because of the nature of the disabilities of the children, more than a full-time faculty would be necessary. Many of these youngsters are incontinent of bladder and bowel control; just the problem of caring for their toilet needs required the attention and devotion of a volunteer group. Realizing this, I felt also sure that there was a group within the community on whom we might call—a reservoir of women whose own families had grown up but who had the requirements and experience to become assistants to our faculty.

I talked this over with the Rev. Dr. George Parker, of the Manhasset Congregational Church, one of the most active churches in service work for their parish and community. Dr. Parker arranged for me to meet with Mrs. Schramm and Mrs. Robinson, two of the leaders of women's groups within the church. A meeting with a large group of the ladies was held later in the church auditorium.

I told them of our plans, our children coming in that fall, the importance of what they would be doing in the enriching of the lives of these children. There were many questions, much excitement. I asked if they would join with us to place their arms around these children who were coming into the world for the first time, to love them as we did and to help us. I told them we would found our great school out of love for the children who would come to it and thus enrich our own lives. For loving means to love that which is unlovable or it is no virtue at all. Forgiving means to pardon the unpardonable. Faith means believing the unbelievable. And to hope means hoping when things are hopeless.

When I invited them over to see Abilities and go through our buildings, they took me up on this, coming in several sizable groups.

The women began to volunteer. Mrs. Schramm and Mrs. Robinson worked out schedules, so that the faculty would be able to devote itself exclusively to teaching; the volunteers would handle all other problems, including recesses and tours of visitors. If any volunteer did not show up as scheduled, she provided a replacement. Once they had signed up, these children were their job; every assignment would be carried out.

Mrs. Schramm's background and training was typical of the average in this remarkable group of women. She had never taught before but she had a degree from Hunter College. At the time she began with us she had one son in graduate school, one in college and another a senior in high school. She knew a lot about children—especially boys! But she had free time now, and she had a deep interest in young people and in service. Anyhow who was to know that out of this might not come a great writer, a great scientist, a great person who might otherwise be lost to the world. As she put it, she had some love to spare.

Dick Switzer was slightly alarmed when I first men-

tioned the volunteers. He even discussed the matter with
Frank Gentile and Bobbi Housman and they came to me
with great consternation: "Hank, what are we going to do
with all those volunteers?"

I told him, "Dick, in this Human Resources Building we
have limited teaching space; much of it has to be done in a
single room. How are you going to carry out this job, take
care of the children and meet their needs, without some
kind of help? This is the only help we have available."

Dick changed his mind about these volunteers before
the first week of actual classes was over. They not only
learned the program and requirements of the school, they
organized under their chairman so efficiently that none of
their problems, getting a substitute at the last minute, for
example, when a volunteer failed to show up—ever inter-
fered with the smooth operation of the school.

The volunteers have become a warm and intimate part
of our faculty. The husbands have become so interested
that they are threatening to form an auxiliary corps.

What do they do? According to the women, "You'll do
almost anything. Help Ronnie with her reading, take Janie
to the bathroom, make valentines with the little ones, feed
Gary, conduct tours for visitors; volunteers can be expected to do anything from toileting or feeding to mopping
up or mothering, writing a letter for a youngster, helping
with a French verb construction or a science lesson or
taking some little boy with a nosebleed into the medical
office, hurrying along the corridor and saying soothing
words and trying to staunch the flow of blood at once."

Yet each comes at it in his own way. Juanita Miller, for example, another volunteer, told me how she felt at first; she came in as a volunteer a few weeks after we had started classes:

"And of course, I remember Gus so vividly because he was strapped flat on a board at that time and he had very little control, and they asked me to sit by him to keep him from hurting himself. They were having a French lesson and Gus was so excited when he knew the answer to something that he really was beside himself, and I remember how strange it was when he said to me, he wanted to answer a question, 'Would you please raise my hand?' And now, of course, you can see Gus and what he has learned and can do . . . "

But it was quite another story in those weeks just before the actual great experiment of this school began. No one was quite sure how any of it would work out. We had gone through our roles in rehearsal a dozen times. For each of us it was in some measure a moving experience; emotions ran deep. Would the buses arrive to pick up the children and get them to the school? Would our textbooks show up in time—many of them hadn't and many of them didn't. There was needed furniture, textbooks and supplies beyond what the Vocational Board could provide.

And the children themselves, for many of whom this would be a first time in any school, a first time on their own, away from their parents and the protective walls of their home environment—how would they meet this experience?

In the summer of 1962 and in the midst of this tempestuous action—carrying on the work at Abilities, running the camp for the children, planning feverishly for the new school opening and the hundreds of details that had to be taken care of, an unexpected development entered the picture, one no one could have anticipated.

A telephone call from a state official came one late afternoon to inform us that we were to have a visit from the Governor, Nelson Rockefeller.

In Albany he had heard about this summer camp and the unique school we were about to start. He had heard about Abilities.

Governor Rockefeller was to be in the area and wanted to see for himself exactly what we were doing.

Chapter 9

We had been given no forewarning of this call or this sudden visit. We did know that the Governor and some of his associates were making a speaking tour in the down-state areas of New York. I had heard that he would be briefly in Nassau County, to make a speech or two and meet with local leaders.

Certainly our school could use his backing. We were technically not a school in our own right—only a unique kind of landlord. We were leasing temporary quarters in the Human Resources School to the Vocational Board.

That was the situation even though we were in fact doing all the basic work, putting this together with infinite care and faith in what we were doing. The Vocational Board understood this, although they did not in any sense surrender their fundamental responsibility. Improvised, jerry-built as our relationship was, with the asserted problems of jurisdiction and authority and who does what and who gives orders to whom, they have our eternal gratitude. Without them, there could have been no beginning for this school.

102

Ultimately I wanted a school run exclusively by us, not using improvised classrooms, not run technically by the Vocational Board or anybody else, but run by us in a building designed as a school, designed for the needs of the children we were bringing in, designed to formulate a wholly new type of education.

This was my dream, even as the call came telling me about the impending visit of the Governor.

But it was hardly the moment to bring it into any conscious focus. The beginnings were all ahead of us, the mere matter of being officially born as a school at all. And the Governor was on a very crowded schedule, we were duly notified. He had other important calls to make.

Half an hour exactly, the lady who called explained. "I'm sure you understand. It's just that, well, he is terribly rushed and it'll just have to be a flying visit this time. But he is so anxious—"

She gave us the precise time according to the schedule worked out. As I recall, he was to arrive at Abilities at 2:00 P.M., Friday afternoon. Departure for his stop on the day's itinerary: 2:30.

"So if you will just alert all your people there . . . "

We were alerted. Preparations for this unexpected visit from the chief executive of the state were underway.

Coming as it did at this tenuous moment in the development of the school, the Governor's visit loomed as having special significance. I was aware that he was on a political speaking tour; the reporters and photographers would be along; perhaps it was only for the Governor one more baby-kissing call, news photographers demanding one more profile of the Governor, a youngster in his arms. But for us I hoped it was more, a symbol of a kind of recognition, of official awareness.

Half an hour, I thought.

It was hardly enough to see the place, really, but we would have everything ready. Orders went out to keep everything active and in operation, so that the Governor could catch the working spirit of Abilities, the research work at Human Resources, and the strange excitement of the handful of wonderful children in that second "camp" program.

"He'll want to see our kids in the pool, of course," I told Switzer. "And a music session—singing—that ought to be interesting . . . "

Dick passed along the word. The camp would be in full swing; the youngsters in the pool, the children in a regular music session, singing.

I don't know how many times the children in that room went through their renditions of "Frère Jacques," "Alouette" and "America the Beautiful." It seemed to me they started singing again every time a car went by outside or a motorist honked his horn.

And the children getting in and out of the pool were gradually becoming, I was certain, more and more waterlogged.

What with the children singing, the youngsters dragging themselves in and out of the pool, the heat of the summer afternoon and the general tension through our entire organization, it was a long wait.

The Governor's cramped program was simply too much for any one man to follow. He was almost two hours late at Abilities when a state trooper showed up and ordered Johnny, our one-handed Abilities chauffeur, "Get that station wagon out of the driveway."

Johnny didn't quite understand what he meant. "Look, officer," he protested, "this is private property—and besides, that's the boss's car."

"I don't care whose car it is," the officer informed him firmly, "the Governor is on his way. The driveway has to be cleared." Johnny apparently is not impressed by state troopers. "I'll move it," he said, "but the boss may not like it." He moved it.

By this time impatience was at a peak. The youngsters had been practicing their singing to a point where some of them were hoarse. We were almost ready to send the waterlogged youngsters back to the lockers to get dried out and dressed. Then we had another phone call: "The Governor will be there in five minutes. But he's terribly late and he can't stay one second over the time allotted. We all hope you'll understand."

We understood. We could hear the siren in the distance.

We were waiting outside when the entourage showed up. Entourage was the word—and the reason why the driveway had to be cleared: There were some forty cars in the parade. There were state officials, photographers, newsmen, local political leaders—the whole typically-

American galaxy of an afternoon of business and politics, full of excitement, high pressure and exuberance.

The Governor was pleasant, smiling, interested from the start. But obviously this was only one more place that was reaching out to him for attention. It was a rushed day, he was one man, there is only so much energy in any human being.

We shook hands, went through the formal introductions. Because of the hurried schedule, we began at once the tour of Abilities.

It was then I began to note an immediate change in the Governor's whole manner. What had been perhaps just one more routine call they had suggested he make began to reach him personally, in a very special and obvious way. His whole attention and interest and concern was caught up.

This was handshaking with workers not of the usual sort; some of the hands held out to him had shining steel hooks in place of fingers. Some were only stumps.

He met Alex. He met our vice president and general manager, Art Nierenberg. He met many workers in wheelchairs, on crutches, workers doing jobs that many would think impossible—making precision components, working on delicate electronic equipment—others doing the "harness" work of wiring plane sections, some of them producing the most delicate equipment for such things as dictating and advanced medical electronic equipment.

Watching these hundreds of men and women at work, people who refused to surrender their lives and dignity and productivity merely because they had some physical disability, the Governor was obviously deeply impressed. These were the people who preferred the challenges of life to the guaranteed existence.

This was patent in his manner, his questions, his detailed interest as he would pause to talk with this one or that, asking about their particular job.

But the minutes were ticking away and the children were still waiting in the other building. . . .

And it was when the Governor came into the Human Resources Foundation building—the "summer camp" area —and saw the children that the impact on him had its full effect.

He came into the large recreation room where the children were gathered with the music teacher, Mrs. De Mott, in her wheelchair. With his usual geniality he bent down to hold one of the youngsters for a moment, to speak to this one or two, smiling, and one of the little girls, standing erect on one crutch, said very positively, "Mr.—I mean Mr. Governor—we've been waiting to sing a long time."

The Governor joined in the laughter at this firmly uttered comment. He apologized to her and the others for having been held up so long. "You know how the traffic is. Besides, I have to stop and shake an awful lot of hands along the way."

There was a chorus of general consent at this. The young lady, however, persisted. "But we are waiting to sing, Mr. Governor."

"And I'm waiting to hear you," he told them.

And so they sang for Governor Rockefeller and his entourage. They sang two songs—"Alouette" and "Frère Jacques." The pronunciation was perhaps not the most perfect French ever sung, and the music may have been occasionally off key—but the Governor stood there listening, the photographers took many pictures, the newsmen, the State and local officials standing behind the Governor, with the children in their chairs and on their assorted crutches and braces, standing and singing.

It was a remarkable climax for them to that long day of waiting, these erstwhile hidden children singing for the Governor.

Finally he saw the children in the pool.

He stayed there watching these children, legless children, youngsters with withered arms and hands and feet, with twisted deformities, yet here, under our physical therapy program, they were strengthening muscles that otherwise might never have had a chance to develop.

"Be careful, Governor," one of the boys in the pool called. "We're liable to get you all wet with our splashing."

"Don't worry about that," the Governor called back. "I'd like to be in there with you right this minute."

For some time he stood watching the youngsters swimming, diving, floating, playing, splashing water at each other—shouting, unafraid, unselfconscious.

Time was running short. But Governor Rockefeller and his group found time to look at the bowling alley specially built for our disabled people, with special equipment for rolling balls. He watched one of our children bowling. He examined in detail the equipment used, listened with delight to the stories of Alex's victories not only here but outside on regular bowling alleys—Alex who holds a full-sized bowling ball in his two eight-inch shoulder arm stumps, averages 155 a game.

He also took time to go through the Human Foundations building itself, the auditorium that holds four hundred people, the telemetering research equipment developed by our scientists for medical research into energy expenditure, the laboratories for research in bioengineering, prosthetic, medical and psychosocial investigation, our library, the data processing facilities, as well as the rooms we were already setting aside as classrooms for the school that was soon to start in the fall.

Time was running short. But when we came back to the main building and reached my office, the Governor informed me that he was throwing overboard the itinerary for the next hour or two. "I'd like to talk a little more with you, Mr. Viscardi," the Governor said. "I'd like to have a chat with you—perhaps Joe and I could come into your office."

He indicated Joseph Carlino, the Speaker in the New York State Assembly.

So they came into my office and the three of us talked. We told him about Abilities, our Human Resources Foundation and the school. These were pilot plants to show all the world a new attitude, a new approach, a new meaning and dignity for millions of disabled humans—people who preferred to support themselves.

During the course of this conference the Governor said, "What I have seen here is one of the great accomplishments of this country. I'm tremendously impressed by it, by your work and your plans for the future. I'm deeply moved by it."

Carlino said, "It is a very moving experience, Hank, to see these people, particularly these children."

Sitting in the chair beside my desk, Governor Rockefeller asked, "What can we do to help? How can I, as your Governor, help you in your work here?"

I had not anticipated this direct approach. After all our struggle here was Governor Rockefeller asking what he could do for us and these children. He was putting aside other important matters and appointments—the half-hour limit was long since past and forgotten—to hear our story.

I began to tell him our story, our complex setup, the confusions of control and direction, our need for a school of our own, how we understood from the lessons of our own lives the need of a school chartered solely as the Human Resources School.

"We need our own school building, one specially designed to meet the problems of the severely disabled children, the most severely disabled, to give them a chance for a full education and life."

Designing such a unique school building, planning it, funding it, this would be our responsibility; the school itself, the charter, the right to run such a school ourselves

—this we needed. "We feel, Governor, that this could be a tremendous pilot demonstration for the State of New York and for the nation, and if you can do anything to help us achieve this goal, I'll be deeply grateful. Perhaps if we build the school the State could help with the tuition payments for the children."

The Governor turned to Carlino: "Joe, what do you think we can do?"

Carlino said, "Well, I don't know what form it takes, but I would imagine it requires something in the way of legislation. I believe in it."

"Will you take care of the details, Joe?"

"I'll look into it right away, Governor," Carlino said. He turned to me. "Give me a call, Hank, in a day or two? You know this is my home base, this part of the world."

He puffed on his cigar. A very fine looking man, Mr. Carlino.

The Governor was standing and smiling and we were shaking hands. Then suddenly he was gone. They were all gone.

Chapter 10

||||||||||||||||||||||||||||||||||||||||||||||||||||||||||||||||||||||||||

But such plans as these did not come into reality quickly.

It was not to be any overnight transfiguration. It would be not weeks but months before any legislative action could be attempted. We knew also that there could be strong opposition from other groups to whom such a charter would be invaluable.

And meanwhile, the school for these children, with all its improvisations, was about to open. On that third Thursday in September, 1962, they began to arrive for their first day in a classroom.

The confusions of that opening day were multiplied many times over by the whole organizational setup. Our relationship with the Nassau County Vocational Education and Extension Board was a bewildering one for all concerned.

Dick Switzer was to us at the Human Resources Foundation the head of the school. To the Vocational Board he was listed only as a teacher; the Board was running the school.

This was all well and good except that our needs outran what the Vocational Board could supply. They were overburdened taking care of assorted groups that came under their jurisdiction—retarded children, brain-damaged children, the emotinally disturbed and other groups requiring special training. Their problems ran into the thousands; we were only twenty-one pupils.

But they paid most of our teachers' salaries and much of the costs; they in turn received payment from the school district for each student we took in; they were in charge, officially.

Everyone at the Board did his very best for us. They had a multitude of problems to deal with of which we were one item along the way. But because of the nature of this school and the meaning we saw in it, the promise it could hold to tens of thousands of nameless, confused children, these hidden children of the world, it loomed far greater to us. The Board was extremely concerned with safety provisions. It was they who suggested we put nurses on the buses. We disagreed because we felt that the more independence the child could get, the better. They agreed to this; they were wise, I think, in leaving to us most of the ultimate planning and policies, the actually carrying out of the program. They soon left us to run our own program. There was much elsewhere for them to do.

Dick also had begun a running battle to get his supplies, which had to be ordered through the Vocational Board— textbooks, paper, pencils, furniture, the thousand and one items required to put a school into operation. The Board's rules and regulations sometimes seemed puzzling to us; for example, they would provide furniture, desks and chairs, they said, for the main classroom but only for the pupils; the teacher's desk was not included. They didn't consider that an "essential" item!

However, as late as a week before Labor Day, nothing had arrived, not one piece of furniture. Then we got word that they were sending us regular school desks—but a wheelchair cannot fit under such a desk. We needed adjustable table tops for these youngsters of ours and we put in orders with a seating company for the type we needed; in fact, we set up a policy of buying whatever we needed and paying for it ourselves; whatever we got from the Vocational Board was a kind of bonus.

Not all of these desks had arrived by opening day. We used some of the work benches from Abilities to fill in until the real desks were delivered; we had no teacher's desks; we borrowed one from an Abilities foreman. No textbooks had arrived, no paper, no pencils. We were, as one of the staff put it, starting the great dream for these handicapped children with a few minor disabilities of our own.

But we wrote all of it off as the usual opening day confusion. We would make do. We would get the school underway.

Through it all I think I was perhaps the calmest in the face of that turmoil.

After all, somehow children were coming, they were waiting expectantly for the great day; the dream was in existence, breathing, alive.

At that particular moment that was what counted.

Much of the nightmarish alarms of opening day re-volved about the buses for the children. Bids had been accepted and contracts awarded to various bus companies to do the job. This for them was only part of a large contract involving many children. But opening day was a fiasco, with overtones of tragedy; this was the great day, everything had to work smoothly.

Bobbi Housman had been concerned earlier when she learned that many of the bus companies did not have buses with ramps and perhaps did not realize that they were going to be carrying children in wheel chairs. She called some of the companies and explained to them the kind of children they would be transporting.

Bobbi reported to me after these calls, "Well, they acted as though this was just an everyday occurrence with them and who was I to try to tell them how to do it. Maybe I'm wrong. Maybe they do know after all."

That day many of the buses didn't show up. Many of the children were left waiting. Some were brought by their parents in their own family cars. Some just couldn't get to the school at all. Most of the buses had no ramps, children had to be lifted on. In one or two instances they had three or four steps and it was impossible or unsafe to try to lift a child on under such conditions, and the child simply couldn't get on. Some of the buses had been given wrong addresses or could not locate the right ones.

One little girl, Betty, who had never been to school before in her life, waited two hours outside her home—standing outside on her crutches—for a bus that didn't arrive. There was no car available to transport her so she had to go back inside the house. The next day she waited again—for another two hours that wound up in disappointment; the bus driver simply couldn't make it. School started on Wednesday; it was a long weekend before, on Monday morning, the bus finally showed up at Betty's street and they helped her on board so that she could go to school.

Eventually we had to revise the whole operation. We had to make sure they used buses with ramps, we used our own bus in addition and hired our own special school bus driver, Tom, who took upon himself the unofficial chore of checking on all the other buses to make certain every safety measure was employed, the wheelchairs securely fastened while the bus was in motion, the driver properly instructed in handling the child on the ramp. In many respects we might be considered barging into an area which did not belong to us for supervision. We did it anyway.

But that first day the pandemonium which was in full swing by ten or eleven o'clock only increased during the day. Phones were ringing constantly: parents calling to know where the buses were; no bus in sight and what were they to do? Other parents calling to be sure their child had arrived. There were many people on hand trying to help organize things.

To our surprise a psychologist arrived to give the children some tests. Before Dick Switzer even had a chance to greet the twelve children who had managed to reach the school, the psychologist got them together and informed them, "Now, children, I'm going to give you a test."

At this, a number of the children burst into tears. These youngsters had been on home instruction. Tests and examinations were unfamiliar to them—words they may have heard with frightening connotations.

Some of the children had not resolved their physical problems in schoolwork. How would they manage to hold a pencil or turn the page of a book? One six-year-old who had no digital use of his hands was delighted to show one of the volunteers how he could turn the pages of a book— with his nose.

Dick Switzer tried to get this opening day test called off but was informed that the tests had to be given, they were part of the routine; these were the achievement tests that would set the grade system in the school. Some of the children had never been away from home before. In one instance, a ramp had to be built at the front door so that one boy could come out of his house—for the first time. It was a first in so many ways, for them—and us.

The psychologist gave them the regular Stanford Achievement test. It would, we knew, have little validity for our children. After they calmed down, Bobbi and the nurse-teacher quieted a six-year-old who was sobbing in her wheelchair, and another child who was standing in bewilderment, crying and twisting her hands nervously.

The psychologist soon realized the difficulty when he handed one youngster a pencil and realized that she had no arm. How could she take the test? It was evident that special techniques were called for.

But the evaluation tests were given and the youngsters took them. All of us, including the psychologist, knew that they had little real value in measuring what these children could or couldn't achieve, for that had to be measured in terms of individual deprivations each had experienced in learning opportunities.

Even in the sporadic chaos of this first day, we were all striving to bring some order out of the initial impact of chaotic conditions. Mostly the children were withdrawn, quiet, frightened. This was all brand new; there were no old students to greet each other after the summer vacation; it was all new, they and us. The first part of the experience had to be social rather than academic and they were used to the one-to-one relationship with their home tutor. Here it was a class, here were other children.

And in their hearts and minds you knew they were wondering: Will this one be my friend? Will they like me? Will they take me in as one of them?

Dick Switzer made no attempt that first day—or indeed for the first couple of weeks—to launch a formal teaching curriculum, reading, spelling or arithmetic. Everything had to be very informal. It was almost playtime, to a degree: trying to get them into some basic classification, trying to get them to adjust to all new things and particularly to each other.

Many of the children who had never before been away

from home were nervous, cried and wanted to go home; the volunteers were rushing around dealing with one child who needed a moment's mothering, another who needed toileting, a third who had to be helped with some adjustment on a brace that had come loose. Some children came in wearing braces that were worn out, or long outgrown, and of little use; some wore no braces when they should have had them. Two of the children were on litters—sort of reclining wheel chairs. One was Rhonda, the other a chubby little girl they called Laura.

During those first days they began adjustment through letting the children learn in games. Any academic work that was done was done in games, a simple numbers game, for instance; this was arithmetic, at the start. Reading was reading them stories, rather than any formal learning to read—actually the reading textbooks did not arrive until a week or so after we started, so no formal reading program could have been started in any case.

Dick was evaluating the children over these first two weeks, without their really knowing it. Although their ages ranged as high as sixteen, few of them were above a fourth-grade reading level. The few that were above fourth-grade reading were those who had been in a regular school at one time but had been forced to drop out because of their disability in relationship to the school assignments or to architectural barriers in the school building.

One of the first lessons Dick Switzer gave them, during the first few weeks, was their environment: Where did they live? He found that they did not know what state they lived in; they confused state and country, they thought they all lived in a state called the United States. They did not know either that they happened to live on an island called Long Island. When Dick mentioned the Long Island Railroad they wanted to know, "What's that?" They weren't conscious of the Long Island Railroad, that it was used primarily by commuters going to and from work in New York City. They didn't know the word commuter. Dick told me, "I've worked long and hard with disabled children, but I have never experienced anything like this. We have to start from scratch with everything and work our way up."

What these children knew about their environment was the home and the hospital. They knew about New York City as the strange world where they went once or twice to get braces or crutches. Some of them had never been to the city; some had never been out of their homes except for one or two brief occasions. If a child lives in a wheelchair on the fifth floor of a walkup, he or she is not likely to get downstairs often, however much the out-of-doors leaves and grass and sky may call to him as to any child.

How little they grasped the shape of their environment and the customs and activities most of us take so much for granted came sharply into focus when Dick asked them where a glass of milk came from. How was it delivered to the house?

Several of the little girls were certain that the milk was delivered in the glass their mother set before them.

But on that first day he could make no effort at real

teaching. His only hope was to get some kind of order. This he began to do around eleven in the morning by clearing the classroom; no one was allowed in who didn't belong; parents were out, bus drivers—no one except classroom teachers and children. He eventually got everyone out, so he could begin to deal with our children himself, to talk with them individually, to greet them as a class.

Lunch time came. The children ate in the cafeteria that day. It was the first time they had ever eaten in a public cafeteria. They did not know what to do. The teachers had to explain to them what you did, how those in chairs wheeled up—like the adults they saw getting their trays and dishes—and got their food, and brought it back to the table set aside for them. It was a difficult job to learn all this and the staff worked closely with them, helping them, showing them how to do it.

Of course the Abilities people themselves were extremely interested in these children. They had been sneaking down the corridors all day for glimpses of them. In the cafeteria the children were the center of attention and several of the workers gave the children bits of their desert or pieces of candy. We had to put a halt to this because our Abilities workers, who were seeing themselves in these children, would have spoiled them completely.

But Mrs. Fitch, one of the teachers of the upper grade, described to Dick Switzer the sight of Jimmy, one of our spina bifida boys, in his wheelchair, proudly coming back to the table and announcing, "That's the first time I ever got a meal for myself in my whole life. Oh, boy!"

After lunch and a brief play period they went back into their classrooms.

Some of the pandemonium had quieted down now. The workers from Abilities who had found reasons to sneak in for a look at the children were also pretty much settled back at their jobs and workbenches.

The children themselves were very quiet that first day. There were no behavior problems at all. It was too new, too strange, too exciting, too frightening. This was the outside world, and this was their first day in it, their first day on their own as individuals.

But one moment I don't think I will ever forget. I dropped in myself in the afternoon. I must at once confess that I am the greatest patsy of all when it comes to these youngsters. I fill up just to watch them. And I certainly did that day.

I'd been watching them come in—all of us, I think, had kept our calendars clear for the momentous event. But now I saw them as a class—twelve of the school, eight boys, four girls. They were dressed in their very best. I knew that one or two of the children had had no wardrobe at all; these were probably the first school outfits their parents had bought for them. The suits pressed, the white shirts neat, the dresses fresh and gay.

The children were there—the twisted limbs, postures, the roly-poly arthritic child, the thin, toothpick legs of a little girl with Cooley's anemia, the thin, pinched, eager-eyed faces, eager and withdrawn at once, looking out at the world with all their wonder and doubt and questions.

It had been a rough day indeed for all of us, but I had a pretty good idea they had borne it the best.

I spoke to these children, welcomed them to this new adventure we were sharing, assured them that we would do everything we could to help them. Our doors were open to all their needs. And I talked a little about the volunteers and the role they would play.

Standing there, watching them for one moment, I felt a surge of emotion sweep over me. For each of these children was, to me, in part, myself. They were in part so many of the workers at Abilities; so many of the disabled I had met and known. They were individuals: one-armed, one-legged, on crutches and canes, and in their chairs, one with twisted hand, one with no hand at all. The world would try to call them cripples, pity them and reject them; to me they were not cripples at all, they were young human beings with jobs to do, with futures to find, with hope to achieve happiness, marriage, love, homes, families. To me they were all things each of us, disabled or not, dreams to be, in the process of formation.

And unlike so many of the stories I had known, in my own life and those of others, they would perhaps have a preparation for what was to come. That was what they stood for—a new approach to training, to development, to hope.

All of this was in my mind as I looked at these first-day children in our classrooms.

Across the room, standing at the door, I saw Alex. Alex whose lack of arms and legs make it impractical for him to wear artificial limbs—so he goes through the plant doing his job on those stumps of his, three feet of dynamic drive and an unwillingness ever to be defeated. He had lived through it all, the roughest kind of background, and he'd come out with victory, wife, family, home, happiness, a good job, friends, a full, rich life.

Alex was standing there on his stumps looking at this classroom, at these children, the grime and sweat of a day's work at Abilities on his face, half a grin on his lips, and tears streaming down his cheeks.

Part III

Reading, Writing
and Wheelchairs

Chapter 11

||||||||||||||||||||||||||||||||||||||||||||||||||||||||||||||||||||||||||||||||||

But however moving it might be to each of us personally, the school was not designed for adult emotionalism for any of us. It was a pilot plant in learning, in the serious business of education for the young handicapped, reading and writing and arithmetic, spelling and history, languages, science, art and music—education for life, for living.

The assignment held serious responsibility—to give this spool shape, meaning, direction. Our whole effort in meeting this was to strive to put together an extraordinary school in every respect. It had to be that or it would be nothing.

Under the guidance of Bobbi, Frank and Headmaster Dick Switzer we were building a faculty of dedicated teachers, for both elementary and junior high. Each of our teachers had special reasons for giving up other opportunities for this adventure in teaching—and learning.

They came from varied backgrounds, by varied routes and for varied reasons.

Eleanor DeMott is a very good example of the kind of special incentive and drive of our teachers. A gifted and lovely musician, composer and music teacher, Ellie is herself in a wheel chair. At one time she had been on home instruction. Because of her great music talent, she received special attention not only from her musically gifted parents but also from the State Education authorities.

Ellie's physical disability was that she had extremely brittle bones; if a child ran into her in a school corridor she might break three or four bones. But her education at home was far above the normal home education program; when she was eighteen she was able to go to Hofstra University—majoring in music.

During summer vacations, even though she was already teaching music in her home, Ellie wanted to get away from home surroundings, to be on her own a little; she heard about us and took a summer vacation job at Abilities making and lacing cables for airplane panel boards.

When she was graduated from Hofstra in 1961, I said: "Come and work for us, Ellie."

But she wanted to get a job teaching music. This was her life goal.

I told her, "It's going to be hard getting the job you want in a regular school, Ellie. You can get some bitter turndowns. You've had offers but from places you know you don't want. They really aren't good offers. Come to work for us."

"I love Abilities, it's been wonderful for me," she said, "but—"

"Ellie, one day we're going to start a school right here for homebound children," I promised. "Who would know better how to teach those children to understand and love music and get the most out of it than you."

Mr. Nemarich, the science teacher, was another example. When Russ Housman first spotted him, he was earning a very good salary as director of a science program in the Mineola public school district. We had something else to offer a teacher—a tremendous challenge.

Come into his classroom, and you see the techniques he had recommended and continues to use, techniques by which children in wheel chairs, children on crutches, children with limited mobility of all types, can do, can learn, can see; here are slides that once were seen only through the microscope in a classroom; but in his class, he has used modern visual techniques to throw that slide on a screen, enlarged many hundreds of times—in color.

The wing of a beetle, the eye of a fly. . . .

Chemistry, biology, physics were subjects from which even the disabled usually were almost automatically excused, whether their talents and interests went along those test tube paths or not.

To bring science to children who could not have science in regular schools, to give the young man who might one day make one of the great breakthroughs the chance to learn: this became the goal of a teacher of such talent and calibre.

This same approach ran through the staff and faculty. Here was an opportunity to bring the world, to bring knowledge, understanding, participation, to those who were usually left out, to bring these things to these young people not out of pity but out of concern because of who they are—and who they might become.

Letitia Carney, our physical therapist, comes to the needs of these children with the same attitude. The little girl who was going to have an operation to give her more mobility in one arm didn't need any operation after one summer in the pool. This is the kind of attitude Letitia Carney follows: proper physical therapy can change so much for these children, even the most severely handicapped.

Mothers and fathers who were terrified at the thought of their child going into the pool quickly changed their mind when they began to see the results Mrs. Carney is obtaining. Not only can they use the pool and do exercises, but they begin to show great improvement and find the self-realization that comes with such improvement.

For every child there is the possibility, she insists, of physical improvement. Take Vera. If Vera had had proper physical therapy at a far younger age she could have had far greater use of arms and legs. "But we are bringing some use back for Vera," Mrs. Carney reports. "Vera is in a wheel chair now where she couldn't move at all before and was on the litter; her muscles are still tight but she can feed herself now, button some of her clothes. . . ."

The same kind of personal involvement reaches into every aspect of the staff—the French teachers who came to us through the volunteers, Mrs. Fitch and her Piper Cub photo-hopping to bring the world to the kids in her classes in a new visual approach; Dr. Leon Greenspan, our medi-

cal director, who in addition to being head of the children's clinical services of the Institute of Physical Medicine and Rehabilitation serves as associate pediatrician on
several hospitals in the New York area.

He has worked with children for decades, the disabled,
the well, the sick, all needing his help, his guidance. Dr.
Rusk suggested to him, "Hank Viscardi's starting a school
out there on Long Island. I've suggested you as their medical director."

And when he came to Abilities for the first time, and he
met our new staff at the school, for the pediatrician it
opened up new vistas. This was something that hadn't
been done before. Of his first visit, Dr. Greenspan wrote
to me:

"I was very happy about what I saw and what I learned
regarding your plans. For years I've been very interested
in the rehabilitation of the physically handicapped child.
But I'm also very concerned about the education of this
physically handicapped child as well. And when I realized
that you are to have—we are to have—a place where these
children are going to go to school, that is what I was
interested in. And that this child's physical needs will be
met in the same way as a child meets the physical needs
when he goes to gym period in an ordinary school system.

"What is important is that this must not be just another
school for handicapped children. What is imporant is to
make the schooling primary and the physical side must be
just another part of the routine of the school day, swimming, gym, home economics, one more activity. This is the

beginning of giving that child motivation, because learning becomes a purpose of living. . . .

"I went home after my visit to your organization and after hearing this great program I said this is the most wonderful thing that can happen. Experience has shown me that there may be several different methods of treatment of any physical problem and my feeling is, no matter what you're going to do they're going to end up in the same place, if you don't work with them from the point of view of developing their personalities, their interpersonal relationships."

This was equally true with our psychologist. For this we brought in as the school's first consulting psychologist Dr. Edmund Neuhaus, psychological services director of the Human Resources Foundation. He was a man who, like Dr. Greenspan, had a special concern for the disabled, a special understanding. It is not a job for someone who deals with ordinary children as a routine thing. "Our children," Neuhaus states, "do not fit into the routine. Their backgrounds are spotted with areas of difference, areas of disturbance, isolation, rejection by the outside world, retreat, unspoken, fears, longings buried deep, . . . all of this too goes into that little girl or boy you see looking up at you from his small wheelchair with their questioning smile . . . or his tight-pressed lips."

This was a part of the staff we had pieced together in those months to meet this opening day.

For the children, for the administrative staff, for these teachers—for all of us—it was a testing ground. Routines had to be evolved, schedules shifted; every detail could loom as a sudden major crisis and potential disaster.

Phones rang constantly. Almost from the first day, parents were calling with their questions: How was Gary doing, was he getting along all right, was it going to work out? What about homework? When are they going to have homework? I want my child to learn.

For most of the parents this was the first time their offspring had been away from them and their direct authority; they had been largely in control of the educational aspects; the home teacher was there for an hour or so, the parents, usually the mother, had the child the rest of the time. One of the most familiar patterns of these parents, entirely understandable, was seen in a statement we heard many times in talking with the parents of this type of normal I.Q. but physically disabled child. "My child may be physically disabled but he has a fine mind. There is nothing wrong with his mind. He can learn. We want him to learn."

And now that their child was in our school, the big question they kept at us with in these first weeks was: Why don't they have homework like other children in other schools?

Dick and his staff understood and they were patient with the parents and they asked the parents to be patient with us.

Homework would come. Plenty of homework, in due course.

But other matters had to be taken care of first in dealing

with these children, in preparing them for the work that lay ahead.

The children had to be oriented to their new surroundings and new relationships. They had to begin to accept themselves, not as individuals living in a world alone or shunted to one side, but functioning within their capabilities in a going community. They had to accept and recognize and learn about this environment of theirs. When Dick asked them their name, address, phone number, some didn't really know where they lived, the street name or number of their own homes.

"Let's talk about addresses and streets," Dick would say. "What's the name of your street, George? What's the number? What does that name mean? How do you suppose your street got that name?"

And suddenly these children were talking about *their* streets in *their* communities, and suddenly these facts were important and meaningful to them.

Part of the training in those first weeks began with simple things and simple games. They were not used to playing in groups with other children; when they lost they would become upset, often very upset, as if it were terribly important that they win every time. They were sore losers because in their homes they had been able to play only with mother or father and by themselves. Victory was easy, losing was a new and difficult concept. There were even phone calls from some of the parents about this: "Kenny lost today at some game they were playing—he sees it as a real setback."

But they had to learn to lose without becoming upset.

Dick tried various tacks in dealing with this. Sometimes he would change swiftly to some other activity or game, swinging their minds into the new activity too fast for them to have a moment to feel disturbed or sorry for themselves. Or on occasions he would let everyone be the winner. No losers, everybody wins! Or he would tell them, "All right, you lost this one; it's only a game and losing doesn't mean you won't have another go at it. Next time you may even win."

And so gradually with simple, elementary games these children began to grasp the meaning of competition in the world beyond the walls of their upstairs rooms at home.

One of the games was at a third-grade level: Doggie, where's your bone? One pupil is blindfolded and sits in front of the class, an eraser under his chair. Another student takes the eraser, disguises his voice and asks, "Doggie, where's your bone?" And the blindfolded one must guess.

Dick started this with the second and third graders and discovered to his surprise that, baby game though it is, the sixth graders liked it also. They found it a thoroughly delightful activity. As Dick explains it, "For one thing, most of them never played a game like this. It's a new experience, this kind of group activity and participation."

Sometimes they would play some very simple classroom game with a ball. Or a game Dick made up called Eraser Tag—it begins with one child putting the eraser on some other child's head. Or the familiar game played with the lower grades: Simon Says.

All the time that this preliminary adjustment period was

going on, another equally important process was evolving;
we were learning about them, who they were really, what
they were, what they could do, how well or badly they
read, what levels they were at in the various subjects. We
based our program on the New York State curriculum,
modified to meet the special educational needs of our children. It was designed to provide them with a full educational program equivalent to that of all regular schools.

The kindergarten child, for example, who has never
been in school before or had any formal study of any kind
can be taught like any normal child. Disability or not,
they've had no failures yet in life; they've had to live with
their disability since birth and they're adjusted to it. They
really don't realize they're different. They have a good self-
concept and they roll ahead. They even follow a regular
curriculum with nursery rhymes, rhythm games, singing,
drawing pictures, recognition of pictures, and then into
their reading primers.

Sometimes the fact of going to school has an unusual
effect on the very young child in the home life: One of our
very young students came from a large family with several
brothers and sisters, all normal, all doing very well in
public schools. So everyone else always had the praise and
the interest, and Danny, homebound, disabled, naturally
was left out of that part.

One night, not long after school began, one of the older
brothers reported at the dinner table, "Say, my teacher
said she was over yesterday to the new Human Resources
School and she was praising the school to our class and

you know what—I'm a celebrity in my class on account of I have a brother in that school—Danny. I'm a celebrity . . ."

For the first time in his life, Danny wasn't someone to be pitied. Danny was a star.

Techniques of teaching had to deal not only with the younger ones but with the older children as well, those who had already tasted bitter defeats and setback, even in so simple a thing as reading. Reading provides an excellent example of the kind of program our staff faced. At the time we began to work with them, most of the children were about three or four years—often more—behind their chronological age in their school work, most of all in reading.

But how do you catch and hold the interest of a sixteen-year-old boy or girl with a second grade reading level, particularly since many of them had spent most of their waking hours looking at television, absorbing the "adult education" of soap operas, murder yarns and westerns? Are they likely to be interested in the second-grade reading book adventures of Billy and Jane?

Dick and the staff solved this in two ways. First they obtained a series of books that went as low as the second-grade reader. They were selected for the truly poetic in them, the truly fanciful and imaginative. These were animal stories, fantasy blended with the taste of nature. They had an appeal for all ages but yet were written simply enough to meet the second-grade learning levels. Because of this high interest for children of all ages, they became extremely valuable as part of our school remedial program.

We have done a great deal in remedial reading, employing where necessary audio-visual technique and machines. The main approach, however, is motivational; the child must want to read, he must have books available he can read easily, books that he likes.

This is reading motivation—a story the child likes.

But he must find a story he is capable of reading, that isn't beyond him because of words he cannot read or understand. The fact that he can understand a story means that he is succeeding in reading. For the first time he understands what the story is about—and cares—and he reads on.

Our teaching techniques are simple and direct. Both the whole word recognition method and phonics are employed; we want the child to understand and the technique must serve that objective. We let the student sound out the first letter of the word, and the last; to teach him to love to read, there are drills in phonics and word construction but such a drill period should last no longer than ten or fifteen minutes at a time.

One young girl in our school—with a perfectly normal mind but a severely crippled body—had a reading and academic level of the third grade. There was nothing wrong with her mentally, all of her backwardness in schooling was due to the diet of academic deprivation on homebound schooling.

We put her into "third" grade. Before twelve months had past, she advanced five grades—on sheer learning ability!

She told one of her classmates, "Why, I've been promoted more times in this year than some of my friends have been promoted in their whole lives!"

Even in these first weeks of the school, the concept of education for these children had begun to take shape. Their needs were special, yes; this one perhaps cannot ever hold a pencil and must learn to write his name on an electric typewriter. Every child must learn to make some mark as his legal signature.

Here is a boy who can barely lift his hand; how are we to teach him to do an arithmetic problem on the blackboard? The answer is: a special three-foot-long chalk holder. He learns to make figures on the blackboard—it is actually green because this is a better color for the children to look at—and before very long his figures made with the chalk are as clear and neat as those of any other child in the class and, in fact, better than some who don't even use chalk holders.

But special or not, there would be no lack, no educational deprivation. The whole would be a rounded concept in which life and learning, book and reality, classroom subject and the world outside would be blended in the child's consciousness as a single thing. There would be a unity of purpose, meaning and action, to which in some measure he could also contribute.

By the end of three weeks, the school was in full swing: Books, furniture, teaching aids, most of the assorted requirements were in.

The withdrawn, silent, wide-eyed faces of the children had begun to change. In the cafeteria where the children ate at lunch, behavior problems began to crop up.

Two boys, both of them severely disabled, began to have a go of it at the table and Mrs. Fitch had to halt the matter and send them into my office for a disciplinary discussion. I can be pretty severe with them, although Dick Switzer insists that the cookie jar I keep in my office is a complete giveaway regarding my indulgent attitude—a charge I do not deny.

In any case, Dick and his staff were actually delighted that a few behavior problems had begun to appear.

In October, the school had a Halloween party. In Dick's technique of using everything, turning everything into a learning experience, this was no ordinary party. It was what is known as a "unit"—an activity or series of related activities through which the various skills our students were learning in the classrooms were put to work.

Somewhere about October first, Dick made the announcement to the school. "When is Halloween?" he began. "What is the date? What happens on Halloween?"

After some discussion, he announced: "We're going to have a Halloween party. Just what does that mean? What does it involve?"

Preparation and motivation; they had heard of parties.

All of them liked the idea of a party; some had never had one or been to one; none had ever planned a party, or taken part in planning one; always before this was done by mother and father.

Now they would be doing it themselves.

To carry out the project they had to do a certain amount of special reading to find out just what is done at a Halloween party. Dick Switzer brought in a number of books and articles on the subject, game books, party costumes, Halloween stories and ideas. Student committees were formed: a decorations committee, working with the art teacher, Russ Housman, a game committee, a music committee, a food committee, and others. Discussion of the food aspect revealed that few of the children had the slightest notion of where food came from, how it was brought into the markets. Not only did Dick and his staff discover the little girls who thought milk arrived at their homes in a glass—they learned also that only one or two of the children had ever been inside a supermarket or had any real idea how any of the food arrived or from where. So part of the project became a continuation of the learning unit—to find out about food and especially how a supermarket runs, including how you make purchases.

The day before the party we took the children to the supermarket to make their purchases. Each of them was told to bring some money. Dick had looked up all the prices, had gone to the A&P and made the arrangements to bring the youngsters and had obtained a good line on the price ranges. The A&P people were delighted. The manager told Dick, "Look, why don't you let me close down the store and just turn the place over to you and the kids?"

Dick told him no, he appreciated the offer but this was not the idea. He wanted the children to be with the people, to get used to them, to their staring, their comments, to the whole process which was also for them a part of learning to accept—and live.

Just before Tom and the loaded bus left, Rhonda who asked him, "What is it like—a supermarket, Tom?"

Tom tried to explain it as best a man can. "Well," he said, "there'll be a lot of people there, and rows of vegetables, and groceries and meats and milk and people shopping."

Rhonda thought about this a while and finally said slowly, "I hope I like it."

For these children, the experience at the A&P was far more important and exciting than the party itself. They had never before gone through the turnstiles of a supermarket, seen the long aisles of commodities, food, toys, utensils, cereals, fruit, meats. With the full approval of the manager, Dick went behind the meat counter and explained to the class gathered before him in their wheelchairs on the other side exactly how the meat was packaged and shipped and kept in the refrigerating cases. Dick kept stressing prices to them because he knew they had no idea how much a pound of chopped meat would cost or even the candy they wanted for the party, or the apples.

The manager presented them with a large Halloween cake. The children thought this was wonderful; now they didn't have to buy anything. Switzer told them no, they would pass the cake out after the party, but first they would have to buy what was on the list.

Customers watched the children with strange blends of curiosity, smiles and surprise that the children could do such things so well.

They were orderly and well behaved, and they made their purchases according to the items on their lists— apples, walnuts, raisins, oranges.

It was more than a party, even if they did not realize it. This was learning in a dozen areas, it was experience in reading, studying, researching, history, legend, in folklore and in social living, in coordinating, in participation, in organizing and leadership.

The day of the party was a great event in their lives, their first important activity as a social unit. They showed up in their very best. A few of the boys had forgotten about suit jackets and our volunteer ladies ran home and got jackets of their own so that everyone had one and the classrooms were decorated with artwork and streamers and skeletons and witches and there was laughter and music and cake and ice cream, games and ghost stories and dunking for apples, while outside parents and buses waited in the frosty, glowing autumn afternoon.

Life doesn't consist of living in the past or looking anxiously into the future. How good for them to appreciate that life is now, this day, this hour. It probably is the only experience of the kind one is to have.

Chapter 12

‖‖

In our spacious parking lot behind the Human Resources Building, a yellow bus gleams in the morning sun. This is our own bus built specifically to meet our needs: It has a hydraulic lift so that our children can be taken on board in their wheel chairs without any carrying or lifting of the child.

Arrangements for transporting the children to and from school have been worked out with the regular lines—and the schedules are now properly functioning so that no one is being left on their crutches in the snowdrifts. But this bus out back is our own. It was given to us by our friends at the Franklin National Bank and is used in our program of Recruiting and Training disabled workers. Some of the kids called it "the freedom bus" because it takes them on the trips—sightseeing junkets to life.

Those who can climb into the bus to find seats. The wheel chairs are boarded with the hydraulic lift. Tom, our driver and bus overseer, makes sure the wheel chairs are safely fastened and secure. They laugh, they jostle and kid each other. But there is another strange quality not always

144

seen in young children, their readiness to help each other, in any need.

They do this apparently without any real awareness or thought; it is only that they know what the need is, they understand it in a special immediate sense.

As with all typical children, their thoughts center on the moment. They cannot worry about the charter for the school, the question of whether we will or will not get our building, whether we will or will not ever function as an independent school, or continue to function at all. Their world is only the glittering bus tuning up for this trip.

Today is extremely special. There have been other trips on this bus. But this is their first major trip, their first into New York, to Manhattan Island. For some it will be the first time they have been into the heart of New York although they have lived near it all their lives. To others, New York is the place you go to the hospital for another operation, or to get a new set of braces.

This is the school's first visit to the Metropolitan Museum of Art.

Our rule is that all trips taken by the children must have purpose, a learning value and not mere amusement for its own sake. Many invitations come to the school with a purpose merely of "giving these poor children an outing." Our school program has no place for such an approach. However well intended, these invitations are declined.

Our bus driver, Tom, is another one of those special people who found his way to the school. Tom used to drive a school bus in Port Washington, Long Island. Then he heard about us and our school and came over and got the job driving our bus.

"I love these kids, you know," Tom has told me. "I wouldn't drive a busload like that, all those kids talking and yelling, if I didn't feel like that, that I love them, you see what I mean?"

The first time he took the kids out he had some minor difficulties, however. The hydraulic system didn't function well. Two children had to be carried on. And then the bus started out, it began to rain heavily. The windshield wiper wouldn't work, and the horn wouldn't blow.

As Tom said afterwards, "It could have happened to any bus, any time. It just happened to us on the very first day."

The children reacted like all children. They laughed. They thought it was the most hilarious episode ever.

The yellow bus with its hydraulic lift and its load of children moves out of the parking lot into the street on its way to the Long Island Expressway, to the city, to the museum. . . .

The children joke and shout and sing. Janey calls to Connie, "Are you ticklish?" And Connie calls back, "No, I'm Polish."

Everybody laughs.

Who are these children? Take a cross-section of this bus: Here's a boy we'll call Art. He was born with a condition known as arthrogryposis, a disability that affects joints of the body, particularly arms, hands, legs and ankles, so that they become fixed in an unusually distorted position, gnarled, drawn up.

Art spent most of his life at home. His family has treated him with great wisdom and care. Recently he lost his kitten, the kitten was run over. Art saw it lying still on the road, and, as he put it, "So I knew the meaning of what death is."

Two girls sit down together on the seat in front of Art— they have become inseparable friends in school, a little dark-haired girl with braces, a little light-haired child who used to ride in a wheelchair but now is trying to work with braces too, like her friend. Mary and Anna . . .

June across the aisle is about ten. She has dystonia, a neurological disease akin to Parkinson's Disease in the site of pathology; it is very hard for the child to control muscular movement; but Janet has had two operations, she is much better, she works very hard to walk with a cane.

She and another little girl are deeply engrossed in conversation of their own.

A few days before this, June told one of the volunteers, "For the first time I have a friend of my own."

Steve, who was struck down with meningitis at the age of fifteen, who had been a newsboy and a leader in school and had looks and charm and everything going for him, suddenly, at that age, found himself in an isolation ward, alone, not allowed to see anyone. The treatment for meningitis is a nightmare, a tremendous amount of medication and antibiotics given intramuscularly, at all hours of day and night. The child is a pincushion before they're finished.

Steve was left paralyzed with a speech impediment but Dr. Greenspan heard about him and got him into our school and he began very quickly to come out of the shell of shock and despair. By the end of the year Steve was right up there, talking about his future, planning to go to college and become an expert on Russia, learn the Russian language and become a scholar on that country.

Steve's parents asked his teacher, Mrs. Fitch, "Do you think he can ever make college?"

Mrs. Fitch exclaimed, "Steve! Of course, he's going to college. Whatever made you think he wouldn't?"

Today on the bus Steve and Jack and Bill talk about a model Steve is working on, based on a design of Leonardo da Vinci for a counter-weight mechanism of complicated but highly effective design.

There are others on the bus as they head toward the Long Island Expressway and New York. One of those children is Rhonda, with her twisted, paralyzed body and her large bright eyes that look out with such a strange spiritual fire at life.

Dick Switzer and one or two volunteers are along on this trip. One of them comments jokingly to the children as the bus approaches the Queens Midtown Tunnel, "Now remember, we're going under the water. Hold your breath in the tunnel!"

After they paid the toll and went into the whitetiled tunnel, Dick noticed several of the children sitting motionless, slowly turning red, holding their breath.

Quickly he explained that the statement had been strictly humorous; the tunnel was well ventilated and water tight and nobody had to hold his breath.

Everything on the trip was new—speeding past the houses and watching the other cars and trucks on the expressway, the tunnel and its whirling patterns of taillights and cars, the city, the buildings, the drive uptown, Park Avenue, Fifth Avenue, the trees of Central Park.

Several times Tom makes numerous trips around the block because Rhonda in her reclining litter can't see easily. It is hard for her to turn, so Tom turns the bus to give her a glimpse of the Empire State Building, St. Patrick's spires, the horses and buggies at Fifty-Ninth Street and Fifth Avenue, and farther uptown Cleopatra's Needle, the Obelisk in the park.

At last they draw up to the entrance of the museum. Arrangements have been made for them to come in through a lower entrance so that no stairs will have to be climbed. The museum has also allowed use of elevators for the group.

Rhonda takes one look at this entrance to this great sprawling museum that holds a collection of so much of the world and its meaning, its history, its beauty, and Rhonda cries out, "Oh, boy, let's go!"

Every detail of the trip had been planned well in advance. Russ Housman was along to explain meanings of the art. The original plan had been to concentrate on the Egyptian section since this was part of what they were studying in ancient history. But there was no plan to cut them off from whatever they wanted to see.

We had arranged also for the children to eat in the

cafeteria. The staff was very helpful; they all expected the children would sit down and the volunteers and teachers would bring them their food.

Dick Switzer, of course, had no such plan; each step of this kind of trip was to be part of the learning, cultural, academic, factual—or merely in terms of living. The people in the cafeteria were a little surprised to see our children line up, on crutches or their chairs, and go through the line picking out what they wanted to eat, pay for it, transport it to their own tables—including Rhonda.

Furthermore, they did all this quietly, politely, with no pushing or shoving.

They became very excited about the museum. They enjoyed the Egyptian section but Russ Housman also took them in to see some of the paintings on exhibit, including the Impressionists and Moderns, and he explained to them the purpose of some of these works of art, the meaning in terms of shape, design, color and form.

There were the amusing happenings that day too. One of the boys had a crush on one of the girls. He paid for her lunch, which obviously pleased her. But she sat with the girls to eat it, and he sat with the boys.

And then little Janie, walking with the group, passed a nude statue, and her eyes almost popped out and never looking around she said, "THAT MAN hasn't any clothes on!"

And walking through one of the great high-walled rooms with some of the most priceless carpets hanging there in all their beauty and splendor, one of the young girls shook her head and demanded, "Why do they have all those worn-out old rugs? What are they keeping them up there for anyway?"

But to Rhonda it was all beautiful and all hers, each color, each picture, each lovely delicate statuette, each glorious tinted tapestry.

She didn't want to leave. But we had to leave on schedule for the school buses of the various districts waited to pick up the children and bring them home on our return to Albertson.

Rhonda kept shaking her head and insisting she didn't want to leave yet, and there were tears in her bright big eyes. So they all stayed a little longer.

Some of the boys were in with Mr. Housman seeing the armour of the Middle Ages, the lances and weapons of those days.

Rhonda saw the rooms of the past, the richly embroidered furniture, gardens and fountains, delicate vases out of ancient Rome and Greece. To her, each item was a treasure to drink in, to store within herself, the sudden splendor of the world.

One of our volunteers who went on this trip wrote me a note about it:

"Yesterday the Junior High group visited the Metropolitan Museum of Art. Rhonda and I were with the group. It was a wonderful day which began with loud, happy singing on the bus. The children lined up in the cafeteria, wheelchairs and all, made momentous decisions between hot dogs and hamburgers and couldn't resist French fries.

"With bedpan in a discreet flannel bag hanging from her handle bars, Rhonda gazed wonderingly and silently at the treasures. At the entrance to the French wing with its overwhelming opulence she took a deep breath and said, 'Oh boy!' "

There have been a number of other such trips. The children are in a sense old experienced travellers, within limitations. They took a Circle Line boat tour of Manhattan Island. They had a night out at a typical restaurant, with the children ordering for themselves.

One of the most important and exciting of these trips was taken by the elementary school to witness a taping of the Columbia Broadcasting System television show, "The Defenders." They were shooting a courtroom scene that day but they weren't using the jury box, so the children, the volunteers, Bobbi Housman and the other adults on this trip were able to use the jury box as their vantage point to watch the whole procedure, how a show is directed and made and "taped," by the television camera.

Bobbi gave me a report on her reaction to that trip:

"This was my first trip with the children on the bus, taking the place of the school nurse-teacher who couldn't make it—as you are aware, I'm a registered nurse too—but I was a little nervous as to what would be expected of me. We had contacted the studio people and arranged about toileting—they were letting us take over the men's room at the studio. Wherever you go, you have to check to be sure you can get a wheel chair into a bathroom and we had checked that, of course.

"This was a private film studio where they were shoot-ing, up near 125th Street. We were right on time. I must say the cast was just wonderful; all the actors, directors, everybody greeted us and the children in such a wonderful way, they made us feel as if we—the children that is—were the real stars for this day.

"So there we were with all the lights overhead and the cameras and our kids just bug-eyed watching all of this, but so perfectly behaved. I think that is one of the things about our children, they are so relaxed, not tense at all and yet so well-behaved. They sat in the box during the action and never budged, never said a word.

"They saw part of the show as it was filmed, actors in their makeup, in the courtroom scene, just the way they saw it on TV. Then we took them to the lavatory, the volunteers and I, those children that had to have assist-ance, and it really didn't take us too long. We didn't have any problem to speak of. After the shooting was over, they had lunch with the star, E. G. Marshall, and I think I was the one problem—I forgot to bring my lunch. Tom had to run out and get something. We had Pepsi Cola. And E. G. brought some ice cream. We all had ice cream on the set.

"All these children handling that ice cream, all dressed up in their Sunday best, but we didn't have any of the usual accidents we might have expected, no ice cream all over them or anything like that; they are just amazing, they are so quiet and they manage so beautifully. They forget they're even disabled.

"When the ice cream party on the set was over, we bid goodbye to the cast and to Mr. Marshall. But when we tried to thank the people on the show for giving the children such a tremendous behind-the-cameras experience, Mr. Marshall told them, 'No—we want to thank you— and these children. They put on a far greater show than ours. And theirs was for real.' "

Chapter 13

The school wasn't ours, at least not yet. We were under the vocational board and although we ran the school, legally we were only landlords. But the Governor had been impressed and he had made a promise. We must be on our own. We must build a school for all the world to see, a pilot plant to teach others.

I did not believe anyone or anything could—finally—stop us. It simply did not seem possible.

It was on this premise and faith, that I drove ahead, almost blindly, one might think at times; almost too swiftly, perhaps; I don't know. Here were the children, the plan, the program; we could not stop.

We were a high-speed car driving down what looked like a wide open superhighway. We knew our destination. All we did not know was what obstacles lay between us and our goals.

Speaker Carlino of the New York State Assembly was giving us great help in getting the charter legislation into shape and through the legislative mill. If passed, it would make us an independent private school.

But this still had to be passed. As an interim step, I had obtained a grant of $10,000 from the Educational Facilities Laboratories, a wing of the Ford Foundation, for the purpose of developing by research and study the actual plans for the kind of school building which would be architecturally best suited to our needs.

Already I had begun to talk with people I knew who were interested in our work at Abilities and Human Resources. We would have to raise funds to build this unique structure, this schoolhouse for the young severely disabled of the world—we had friends, people who believed in us.

But while we were a unique school for unusual students, while we developed special techniques in teaching these young people, we did not neglect the fundamentals of basic education, the essential academic requirements. Our curriculum was built around and in accordance with the most stringent requirements of the New York State Department of Education.

Our report on the basic curriculum developed by us for this school states in its introduction: "These children have normal intelligence, but may be academically set back and deprived because of their sheltered environment. They have never socialized with other children and may have adjustment problems. Therefore, the program must pay particular attention to the child's physical and emotional needs . . . our need is for a curriculum based on the adaptations these children must make to participate in a normal society as productive adults . . .

"Our stress, therefore, is on opening up a whole new

world of experience to these previously sheltered children to make them aware of the world in which they live and to develop those skills needed for useful and satisfying participation in that world. . . ."

Need to contribute is something our youngsters seem to understand, far more, in many instances, than their normal brothers and sisters. Having great need themselves, they are more aware of the needs of others.

Our two little incredibles, Tim and George, are examples.

Tim was born with seventeen broken bones; his bones are extremely brittle and he must stay in his wheelchair. But Tim is a driving force of action and promotion of plans; he is a bundle of energy and leadership.

George is the quieter of these two who came to us as kindergarten candidates, five and a half years old. George's bones are fixed in position in arms and legs; he has no use of his fingers. He cannot raise his arms. Using braces he walks stiff-legged. Tim and George are very bright; as the sole two members of our first kindergarten class, they became inseparable pals. Tim is the operator; George the dreamer-type. They work together on solutions to George's more difficult problems.

George couldn't hold a pencil and we were debating about starting him at once on an electric typewriter we use for children who for physical reasons cannot learn handwriting.

Tim and George got together in earnest conversation.

Pretty soon Tim wheeled over to the elementary grade teacher and told her, "I need a sharpened pencil and some rubber bands, please."

"What for, Tim?"

"I'll show you in a minute—if it works!"

When he and his pal George came back their eyes were gleaming with excitement. "Look!"

George held up his stiff arm to display the ingenious plan Tim had devised: George had a well-sharpened pencil fitted and held to his wrist and hand by five rubber bands. "See," Tim explained, "now George can write—he can write by just moving his arm back and forth, up and down."

That afternoon, George wrote his name for the first time. It was awkward, almost illegible. But a comparison with the writing of other children of the same age and development indicated that George was at this stage no less capable than of those learning to write.

As result, we held up the plan to teach George to write on the electric typewriter until we determined if he could learn handwriting by the rubber-band pencil-holding technique.

Tim was pleased at the success of his idea but he and George went on to other important matters, rehearsing to give the primary classes a duet in which Tim would strum a home-made guitar and George would beat a drum, using his hands as drumsticks.

The essential element we have sought to build in our school philosophy is that of total education; nothing is isolated, each thing has meaning, an application to other things. Mornings are given to the skills—learning to read and write and to spell, to add and subtract and multiply. Latest techniques are employed in all these fields but the goals are the same: Ability to handle the basic tools of learning.

Afternoons are given to the application of these skills through wider studies of history and social studies; here the students use their skills, reading, English, spelling; they do research together, they learn about their community, they work on projects, divide into committees, give reports on the community, on transportation.

Each new area emerges from something that has gone before. Transportation begins, for example, with their reading about trolley cars and what is a trolley car—in today's era many have never seen one. From that we lead into the whole area of transportation, how people get around. To these kids, of course, the vital means of transportation is the wheelchair. And so we talk about the wheelchair, and they study it, they learn the history of the wheelchair, they write away for information to companies manufacturing wheelchairs: We need data because they're going to do a report on these chairs—Who made the first wheelchair?

In the field of art, under Dr. Russ Housman's teaching, they examine the wheelchair as a design, as an object of art, as a functional unit for the disabled, and they ridicule the designs. Wheelchairs are generally very poorly designed and the children know this because they live in them and in their art class they try to design their own wheelchairs.

From this we go into a wider area of transportation, and how it applies to them. How does someone in a wheelchair ride on a train? Some of our children—the spina bifida children particularly—cannot get out of their wheelchairs. How does one ride a wheelchair down a corridor of a train? How about the subways in New York City? They begin to learn that they cannot ride these modes of transport unless they have help, and sometimes not even then. Children who can use their arms and hands know that they have to learn to drive a car. Children who have no hands or who for other reasons can't learn to drive have to accept the idea that they will need a friend to help them.

They learn about plane travel and that they can't ride on certain airlines because those lines won't take wheelchairs. We've taken our children to the airport and on a plane—in wheelchairs. American Airlines did this for them—and taxied the plane all over the field, and let them go up into the front of the plane. There they were able to see from actual experience how they could travel by plane in a wheelchair and that it is difficult at best—and in many instances out of the question.

They learn not only to read and write and spell but through these skills they begin to learn about the world and themselves, about everyday life in their community; they begin to discover the realistic limits and facts on their own—this is what the wise teacher does, he or she lets the students discover these things.

Handled properly by the teacher, the youngsters can reach these realities without emotional involvement. The child says, "Gee, I guess I just can't always ride in a plane."

"Right, Ginny—and what are you going to do about it? Cry?"

The teacher asks this almost lightly. Nobody makes a tragedy of it. The class and the student together face the reality. They'll have to find other means of transportation in most cases—until new kinds of planes are built, or new loading techniques designed.

They begin to understand how these things relate personally to them; they begin to realize the role the wheelchair plays for them; they set up a safety code for wheelchairs in the corridors and classrooms of Human Resources; each student and any adult has to pass a wheelchair driving test which includes navigation up and down a ramp. They made me take this test and I almost didn't pass! I did poorly on the ramp.

Some of the boys begin to "soup up," their wheelchairs, with balloon tires and special wheels.

English and literature are particularly important, especially in Junior High because these children when at home still have a great deal of leisure time, and reading and understanding of literature opens up new dimensions. All communications are vital to them. They study literature, grammar, sentence and paragraph structure, speaking, projection, expression, creative writing and reportorial writing, fiction and non-fiction, and poetry.

Some of the students in Junior High—all journalistically inclined young ladies—started a regular newspaper—the H.R.S. Reporter, with reports that are often newsworthy and illuminating.

"On Saturday some of the Junior High children and the grammar school went to Hofstra University to a football game. For many this was their first live football game. It was full of excitement and fun. There were cheers for Hofstra, hot dogs, and cold weather. Many of the children came prepared for cold weather and those who didn't found other ways to keep warm. Unfortunately, Hofstra lost. . . ."

Here also we need George and Tim's five-year-old answers to the inquiring reporter's query of the very young children as to what they would like their husband or wife to be like:

George: "I want to have a girl that likes me, she has to be pretty, big, big blonde, has to like any kind of ice cream. . . ."

Tim: "She has to be pretty and has to be a girl just like Jane, with brown eyes, green hair, eyeglasses and in a wheelchair. Our house must have a backyard with a sandbox for me and the kids . . ."

The students also published a kind of anthology of student compositions. They called it, "We Wrote Them— You Read Them." Amusing and touching, these stories revealed a lot about the students themselves. One was about a nosebleed, another about Iggy, the cat that was run over, another about a French poodle that was too enormous for the family to keep. One was a brief story by a member of the younger *literati,* whom, I think, may turn out to be quite successful writing television humor. This story reads:

ABOUT FISH

Joe said, "I have twenty fish."

Jim said, "I have fifteen fish."

"I have three tanks."

"I have three too, so we are even."

"We are not even."

"Yes we are."

"No we are not. I have four pumps. You have two."

"I have fifteen guppies."

"I have twenty catfish."

"I don't care. My father is buying me fish tonight and I'll have ten times more than you."

"Do you buy your fish in the pet store do n the street?"

In the junior high school literature course, we use few textbooks. Literature is for the living, out of the books themselves, drama itself, out of magazines, newspapers, journals. Many of our children used to see only a Long Island newspaper, rarely a New York City paper, rarely a magazine. Now, on the junior high level, and on occasion even on the elementary level, they're reading the *New York Times* every day, plus magazines like *Newsweek, Time,* even the more liberal areas like *The New Republic* and *Harper's.* We have complete freedom in this area. And we present both sides of the picture.

Our students are also deeply interested in Shakespeare and in drama. They've been over to Hofstra University to see Shakespearean dramas put on by students there. One group of our children in junior high actually went in to see Richard Burton's *Hamlet* in New York. The children arranged it themselves—with financial aid from their parents. Tickets were seven dollars each; they called the ticket agent and they made the plans, including arranging for the school bus to take them in.

They had only six seats, however, and had to take three standing room; they worked out a plan that between each act the three on crutches who had been standing would switch with three sitting down. They wanted to see this so much that they were perfectly willing to stand on their crutches. But with people seeing them—and with the fact that some people didn't show up—they were able to get seats. By the end of the second act, all the youngsters were seated.

When they returned, with Mrs. Silverblank, the literature teacher, Dick asked them, "Was it good?"

And one of the children speaking for the others declared, "No, not good, Mr. Switzer. It was great."

In each area of our school there has been an effort to achieve the rounded picture, from English to Math to Science.

Our school library is one of the most important aids in the picture. It has grown constantly into a truly fine reference library. Without it, none of the research would be possible, because here we have quickly at hand material of all types—dictionaries, encyclopedias, fiction, non-fiction, biography, history, textbooks and references. The school staff is constantly submitting to the librarian lists of new books needed.

In addition, our children are also using the public libraries. We worked out an agreement with the Shelter Rock Public Library, so that they may use that library for research. At first library officials suggested shutting down the library for one day to all but our children. This we didn't approve. We wanted them to have contact with normal children and adults.

We want our children accustomed to the library so that on Saturdays when they are home they can get to their own library and borrow books. Many never thought of this before—nor did their parents. Dropping a child at the library gives the mother a chance to go shopping for the morning while the child can do his homework right in the library—or if he wishes he can browse and read. In most libraries our children can manage.

For both elementary and junior high levels, the entire school day is part of the curriculum, everything that goes on is a part of learning, even when he goes to the bathroom. If a child needs help going to the bathroom—if he's a muscular dystrophy child who perhaps has no use of his arms and legs, and a teacher or staff volunteer has to help him, has to toilet the child, the child must be aware that this is a part of life he must accept—someone is going to have to help him. We try to train the child to care for himself if possible. Often it isn't.

Here is a little girl who has to be placed on a bedpan. All right—this happens. She cannot be embarrassed by it; it is a part of her life she must accept and live with. Often, and understandably, youngsters are embarrassed to ask for help. Asking to go to the bathroom is a must and we train them in this too. With our spina bifida children we have tried to work out schedules and this works very well except where the children themselves fail to keep undeviatingly to their schedules.

The answer we have found lies in teams—one child checks on the other, reminds him or her of the schedule. It is true that there have been accidents; they have no sensation that this is happening and it is embarrassing to them when someone else spots it and tells them. The embarrassment is good; it makes them realize that this is their responsibility, they must take care of this, every two or two and a half hours.

Putting them on a time schedule has been the best plan but we have had some trouble with the boys. So Dick Switzer held a meeting with some of them; all realized it was a problem; the team system was evolved with their cooperation and the situation was noticeably improved.

Once in the early days Dick called one of the little girls

into his office to go over her grades. This little one had never been in a principal's office. She was so excited she lost all control. We all kidded Dick about scaring the children.

Everything they do becomes part of this training for life. In a classroom discussion of food values, we find that some children never heard of a banana split and never tasted one; practically none had ever been inside an ice cream parlor, which is becoming rarer in the American community. So this is put on the schedule: One field trip to ice cream parlor.

Their reading of magazines and newspapers opens areas many had never thought of—art, music, Lincoln Center, the World's Fair. Problems of history open the issues of race prejudice, segregation and integration; minorities are studied and discussed. They know that they, too, are a minority, that some people don't like them, don't like to look at them, because they are different.

They realize that they, too, have to stand up for their rights as citizens; they have a right to live—an obligation to become good, useful, participating members of their world and their community.

Some of our Junior High children are getting together and going to a movie on Friday or Saturday night, going to dances, entering activities in their local churches. This was not often permitted by their parents who were naturally concerned. Their normal parental reaction was: "Oh, my little child can't do this sort of thing; he's crippled."

Now they are learning that he or she can do this sort of

thing, and the worries that they have as parents become no more or less than all parents of adolescent children trying out their wings. Plans are underway also in our school for a full-fledged driver-education program. This will require special hand controls and driver modifications such as Abilities people use.

In addition, we have special training our children need and are getting. They must have a therapy program. This replaces gym. A whole new curriculum must be developed for them in the field of adaptive physical and recreational therapy.

They must have home economics. Boys and girls have to learn to reinforce their clothes in sewing so that from sitting in a wheelchair they don't wear out quickly, or to sew in special zippers or other devices they require, so that the brace they're wearing doesn't wear away the stocking or shirt or blouse. In our new building home economics will be taught in our laboratory for everyday living.

Girls learn cooking—from a wheelchair. Boys learn homemaking. How do you repair things around the house in a wheelchair? What are the latest devices? What must they, as consumers, consider in making purchases? They must keep in mind the lightweight frying pan, and gadgets that aid in opening tins. How does one open a can with one arm or no arm? There is an electric can opener that can be operated with one hand.

Religion is another area of education as well as of living. Our children cannot go to church regularly because so many churches have difficult steps that must be climbed.

We have services in the Abilities chapel or the auditorium —for all three major faiths.

It's important that young people learn—even in the elementary school—some idea of comparative religion, that there are different religions, and each must be understood and respected. School districts say to avoid discussions of religion. But if it is the Christmas season and the Christmas holidays, the children themselves bring the question up: What is Christmas—and why?

You can't just tell them it's Santa Claus time and you exchange gifts. You trace it back in history and religion and show how this became a Christian holiday. And by the same token, isn't it interesting that there is a Jewish holiday called Chanukah at the same time? And that they exchange gifts too, in a different way?

With very young children, we do not go too deeply into these questions; only enough to let them know there are other religions in the world. At the junior high level, assuming the child has had some background in his own religion, you can go into the subject of religion in greater detail. You talk about some of the symbols, rituals, the Eastern religions, Buddhism, Hinduism, the Gnostics. We talk of and study and read about the Crusades, the wars that were fought over religious issues, the reasons why people fled England to come to America and find religious liberty, as their conscience dictated.

We want our children, by whatever road they travel, to understand the fact of God and the love of God. We try to avoid and eliminate the idea of blaming God for their special problems, the idea of blaming anyone. We try to instill the thought only of using what gifts, what abilities, they have; each of us has these gifts, each of us has disabilities in one way or another.

We want them to feel that there is for them, too, something beyond themselves to which they can turn in need, in moments of desperation, in despair, when things go wrong, something to lean upon besides mother and father, teacher or doctor.

Yet there is a lighter side. They also learn to live, to latch on to some of the gaiety of the world that they might have missed. Like a slumber party, all the rage in the high schools of the world—and the junior highs—for all the adolescent kids, the girls who spend the night together in talk and Coca-Cola and gossip.

Disabled little girls with their braces holding a wild adolescent party like this?

One of them began when Mary, about twelve, decided to give the party and invite four or five of her friends of about the same age for a slumber party, where they would sit up all night. Of course, they do this on a weekend night, Friday or Saturday, so they can get plenty of sleep the next day.

The first we knew about the plan came when our school volunteers and staff began getting phone calls from mothers of the girls: "Do you know what is being planned? Is it all right?"

It is understandable that they were nervous about such a party. It must be remembered that many of our children are incontinent and have to change or be changed. A slumber or pajama party is not too big a thing in a normal household, but in the homes of these severely disabled children it is a tremendous event, especially when the disabled little girl spends the night away from home—for the first time.

One of the mothers asked us, "Do you think this party is right? After all, our child is really disabled, needs attention. Suppose something should happen?"

Bobbi Housman answered that question. Gently she pointed out, "Well, there is always a phone nearby and I'm certain Mary's mother would feel toward your child as you would feel toward her if her little girl were in your home for the night."

The debate and discussions went on. But it was all only for the benefit of the parents. The children had made up their minds.

One of the volunteers who knew of this and who has a daughter of her own and therefore knows about slumber parties first hand, told Mary, "Now, Mary, every mother is entitled to at least a half hour's sleep during the night so promise me you'll give your mother a half hour's sleep."

So excited were the girls about this party that none of them would go in swimming on the Friday afternoon before it took place; they were afraid they might catch colds or be tired out so they couldn't stay up all night.

They were young girls with very severe disabilities—but their slumber party couldn't have been more typical. It was an all-night go. They talked. They drank Cokes. They listened to dreamy music and hot music and rock and roll on the record player. They talked some more and ate cookies and discussed boys—several had special boys they were interested in.

They had a pillow fight and there was some wrestling on the bed. No broken bones. No disasters. A lot of laughter and screams and similar sounds throughout the quiet suburban night.

The noise didn't matter. Everybody took the party in stride with all the immediate excitement and shouting, and all the wider range of understanding that children don't bother to put into words.

When Mary was talking to the volunteer who had urged her to give her mother at least half an hour's rest during the longest night, the volunteer, Mrs. Miller, asked, "Well, how did you make out, Mary?"

And Mary answered, "My mother said we didn't give her a full half hour's sleep. Just about twenty minutes."

The way the report of the affair finally went: The girls talked, gossiped, quarrelled, wrestled, drank their Cokes and listened to their music until about 5:30 a.m., in the cool, grey dawn. Then—like any other crowd of weary all-night adolescents—they finally went to sleep.

Chapter 14

|||||||||||||||||||||||||||||||||||||||||||||||||||||||||||||||||||||

Eleanor DeMott, our music teacher, has two goals in mind: Understanding and expression in musical terms. To Ellie, each is a part of the other: "When they come into our school they usually are not used to expressing themselves musically. Many haven't had a chance to have music in their lives, in any way at all. They may never have had exposure to real music. . . ."

In music, in art, in whatever form of creativity their artistic talents led them, we wanted these children to have a chance to see, to know, to reach down these avenues of beauty in terms not of paper cutouts but of art, poetry, beauty.

Ellie who had worked at Abilities—and met there the man she was to marry—Ellie who in her wheelchair brought music and song into the lives of the children. "Anyone can learn to sing, somewhat at least, no one is tone deaf."

The singing of the children helped also in the early days to bring these children out of their shells, their wordless, noteless songless silence.

It was not music by rote, music because the curriculum

said there had to be a music course. It had to be meaningful, it had to be enriching, to each of them.

Very early in that first year, she told her students to
bring in some phonograph record—something they considered really good music, something they particularly
liked.

"How about rock and roll?" one of the boys asked.
"Can we bring in rock and roll?"

"Certainly. But only if you can justify it in terms of
musical values."

The records they brought in revealed a remarkable
range of interests, from Judy Garland singing "Over the
Rainbow" to folk music from the Ozarks, Italian street
songs, one rip roaring rock and roll number, brought in by
a handsome lad who, like myself, has only stumps for legs.
One little girl brought in "My Heart Belongs to Daddy."
There was one opera number "Un Bel Di Vedrenio" from
Madame Butterfly, where the Japanese girl sings of how
one fine day her lover will return.

That was brought in by Rhonda. She didn't know the
story, what it was about, and, of course, the words are not
in English. All she liked was the way it sounded.

I was surprised that Rhonda picked this aria from *Butterfly;* she seemed to have good understanding of it. She
said that the music was beautiful, the melody made her
feel good—that was the way she explained and felt it. Her
mother had said that she likes to listen to music. Rhonda
doesn't sing too easily herself, but she wants to, and has a
terrific desire to sing.

Singing becomes a must in these courses, part of their routine and their lives, particularly in elementary school. And playing instruments: Ellie makes them practice on various instruments, they must understand something of musical composition, even counterpoint. The children seem to grasp complex ideas with remarkable clarity and speed.

In the junior high classes they take up music history, from the Baroque period down to modern serious mid-century music. This study blends into other courses and areas of learning—history, drama, painting.

She will tell her class, "Today we're studying romantic music styles, now—what else was going on during the same period?" She will have them study economic and social and artistic conditions of the age, who was painting, who was writing, to discover how the music fits into the pattern of an era. Above all, she insists that they learn to listen; for any research project, all the records required are available, and record players, right in the school. In one instance, each student was assigned a different composer to "research." They had to learn everything they could about that composer, what he wrote, how his work reflected, or failed to reflect, the period in which he wrote. It was a difficult assignment, much of it had to be interpretative opinion. But in the process they were learning to probe in depth, to reason, to feel and think and respond to the music they heard.

A few of these erstwhile homebound children have special musical gifts. One boy came to Ellie with a great announcement: his parents had given him a guitar for Christmas, and he was going to learn how to play it. It happens that this boy's hands are in a fixed position; his middle finger and his thumb curled and rigid. He could not possibly strum a guitar in any normal fashion. "But I can still play it, Miss DeMott," this boy insisted.

He brought the guitar to show us how he did this. He couldn't hold the guitar and play, but he could lay the guitar face up on the table, strumming with one hand and pressing the strings down with the other. He could only play a couple of strings at a time, but it was all right—he and Miss DeMott were able to work out a way in which he could make it sound very good.

This boy actually is a very good singer and sings folk songs, and the guitar makes an excellent accompaniment to these songs. Ellie says he has a fine, beautiful voice.

As part of her course our students learn to do what is called "directed listening." They listen for certain special things, harmony, counterpoint, rhythm, mood, the purpose, the form. It may be a Bach fugue—which, contrary to general opinion, the children enjoy greatly, or a symphony, modern or classical.

On the record player a Debussy prelude is played, *The Clouds*. The class is silent, listening. Ellie has told them, "close your eyes, see what you see in your mind. What does the music bring into being for you? What kind of scene? What feelings? What is it like where this music goes?"

They are imaginative kids, they have lived alone so much that their imaginations work overtime.

Each one reports in his own way. Each has his own interpretation and imagery:

"It is a lonely scene, there is really no one there . . . only one person. . . ."

"It is sky, it is the sky itself, as if you were transported there, all the white sky. . . ."

"It is a piece of quiet, moving around a little. . . ."

"It's a cowboy riding a big white horse like a dancing cowboy horse in the middle of the big clouds. . . ."

Dr. Russ Housman, our art teacher, takes an approach of the same sort—in reverse. What color is a sound? What shade is a scream—orange, yellow, white, violet, vermilion?

What linear line would a scream take, a bell ringing, laughter, or someone playing an Hungarian dance on the piano?

Each teacher searches out the minds and hearts of his pupils by teaching them to search out their own ideas and meanings for themselves.

Russ's background in art is quite extraordinary—he has had one-man shows in New York and other art communities and he has been widely acclaimed as one of the young modern American painters. Art was always his career, as music was with Eleanor DeMott, although unlike her, Russ is not disabled.

As a boy of eight Russ won an art school scholarship.

He even went to art school for two years—in the afternoons after regular school—without his mother's knowing. She thought he was playing with others on the street outside.

She did notice that he came home often with drawing pads, and finally she demanded to know where he was getting the money to buy these pads. He had to tell her he was going to art school and explained that he got the money from working on a bakery truck early in the mornings, delivering loaves of bread.

She demanded to look at the drawings. This was a regular art school and there were a number of life studies from the nude. His mother was never the same.

Eventually, Dr. Housman went on to Buffalo University, and from there into teaching art in the public schools, coaching the football team on the side. During the Korean War he taught in the Psychological Warfare School, then taught at Hofstra and Adelphi—where he met Bobbi who was to become his wife. Still working on his doctorate degree, he transferred to Milliken University, as head of the art department there. Ultimately, he returned to New York to complete his doctorate, teaching art in the Nassau Community College and agreeing later to work part time for me as art teacher at the Human Resources School.

He has a real affection and understanding of disabled people. For our children, as Russ sees it, art serves many purposes. It can be an outlet. Some educators report that when the art class comes before the math, the boy or girl does better than if the order is reversed. Art gives relief to inhibitions. The boy who has quarrelled with his Dad paints him in black, the death color; he gets the hate out of his system, the need to express hidden emotion, perhaps unknown even to himself; in the drawing he breaks the spell of the emotional disturbance inside.

A boy who can never become a skier in real life draws a picture of a skier, at the top of a hill, about to start down the long slide, about to make the jump, perhaps poised in midair in the midst of the jump itself. He can never do any of this but certainly one function of all art is to bring to reality what cannot be brought to reality in any other way. Such a motive is not a primary purpose of art in any form, in our school or elsewhere, but it is one purpose that can apply particularly to us.

Under his teaching our school's philosophy does not agree with the widely accepted notion of some that the disabled child has to have only a watered-down art program, the pretty postcard type of program. Dr. Housman does not believe in running a disabled art program for disabled people, adults or children.

"This is a program for children," Russ insists. "A program that we hope will develop creative insights, will give them areas for problem-solving, which may lead to vocation or not but will surely make for a richer life."

Our art appreciation programs help them understand their heritage, their cultural heritage, the great art of the past and their relation to it. We don't hide the fact that Toulouse-Lautrec was terribly, terribly disabled, probably as badly as any one of our children, and it didn't keep him from having an artistic genius. We know also that El Greco had a terrible visual disorder yet became one of the world's greatest painters.

We don't dwell on the fact that some of these people, the great artists and musicians, have been disabled but on the fact that they were as they were and yet have left a great heritage for us to appreciate. This leads to the obvious, most important implication: They can do the same, they also can contribute.

Because Russ refuses to let the impediments limit his scope of teaching, he infuses in the class the challenge and motivation to find a way. Part of the art course involves clay working, vase making, ceramics; the classroom has its own kiln. We have gone in for something we call small hand ceramics. One form of this is to take a small piece of clay and let the child form a round ball of clay with his thumb; this is a form of art and finger exercise creativity, valuable where finger action is curtailed.

The potter's wheel is also valuable. One of our older youths had the use only of one hand. But to throw the clay on the wheel and shape it as it turns required two hands—one serves as a guide in molding the clay on the outside as the wheel turns, the other shapes on the inside. The boy with only one good hand borrowed a plastic spoon from the cafeteria; he uses the spoon for shaping on the inside; he can hold the spoon braced in his bad hand. The spoon becomes his finger.

Dr. Housman is constantly urging them to inventiveness

to get around the impediment; he also urges them to develop all their sensory perception. Just as he talked of the colors of sounds, so he experiments in the sense of touch. One day he brought into class a mystery bag. Each student had to reach in and pull out objects with their eyes closed. We made them tell us what this object was—and then tell us in words how they knew this from the sense of touch.

In the museum trip programs, he now gives lectures beforehand—five lectures to provide background information, ideas, stimuli. Russ explains not only the great classic painters but delves also deeply into the meaning of the moderns, down to such controversial painters as Jackson Pollack, for example. Russ knew Pollack briefly before Pollack's tragic death in an auto accident. He explains to his young people meanings in the seemingly meaningless pattern which have so exasperated some and so beguiled art lovers.

Pollack was looking for a kind of sub-microscopic world," Russ tells his class. "One that is right in front of you all the time, always with you but rarely observed. If you lie down in a field of flowers and look through that wonderful tracery of growth, really stare through it and take a photograph of it, and then look in the same way at a Jackson Pollack, you find many of the same kinds of magnificent explosions of growth, of color, of sprawling line and delicate filigree lacework.

"People so often say that Pollack had nothing in mind. This is unfortunate because he did, because he was saying something very earnestly and the failure of the world to even try to understand him may have been a conscious causation of his death."

Strong, even rather daring words, from an art teacher, about a highly controversial non-conforming abstractionist.

But in his next class he will tell them also of a wholly different area of art—things around them, the alphabet, signs, trademarks. He will explain how a monogram is a personal trademark. He assigns the class to come in with trademarks they themselves design for various companies, Ford or General Electric or the Volkswagen car.

We're finding out new things about children and their drawings—for instance, that contrary to generally held pedagogical opinion, kindergarten children *can* work as a team together, even in committees; one Thanksgiving story, painting, for example, was done in the art class by a kindergarten "committee" of four young artists. It was a brilliant well-coordinated painting approximately four feet wide by ten feet long, a true juvenile mural.

We're finding out that the tools of art are actually extensions of the human being. These children, although seriously disabled, can learn to manipulate the materials. They don't have to be babied or coddled. The children themselves have answers—creative solutions—to so many of these problems.

Beyond the artistic field is the psychological. What does the painting mean in terms of the child? If we get him to stop drawing children in wheelchairs, children with crutches, if we can get this boy or that girl out of the dark blacks, the deep brooding purples into lighter, happier tones, into the normal world of the non-disabled in their drawing—can we interpret this to mean that psychologically he has lifted himself out of the shadows, that he has accepted himself, accepted the world, and is ready for it, ready to meet it only on equal terms, when he can draw what we call a normal physical schema? Does this mean adjustment to his disability? Or should he continue to draw the disabled since he is one? Is he only hiding something, avoiding an issue by ignoring it in his painting?

This is another avenue of research that our school and its students and their work may assist.

With our students, all we can do here is to be provocative, not to give answers but to present problems, artistic questions that will develop judgment, understanding, taste, problem-solving that will help them to live a richer life, pick better products, decorate a better home, see a better landscape, appreciate the colors of the sun or the shadows by the tree, the ripple on the lake, and maybe make relationships, as we try to do, between the ripple on the lake and Clair de Lune.

We believe we are uncovering important new guidelines to art education because of the extraordinary experiences we have had with very severely disabled children and what they are doing.

When the little girl on the litter, Rhonda, made her first

drawing, one of the visitors almost threw it out, thinking it a bit of scrap paper. It was a picture of a lady waiting for a bus. But it revealed so clearly the paucity of Rhonda's contact with her world outside herself. For her it was a difficult, complete drawing—made with all the physical difficulties she had to overcome. But it showed only a few straight lines up and down—woman. And a few jagged lines horizontal—the bus.

That was the world. No houses, No streets. No cars. No anything beyond this bleak two-section universe, bus and lady, bleak and empty.

Six months later, Rhonda had made remarkable progress. Her drawings came closer and closer to an acceptable meaningful reality, even if she still had all the difficulty of drawing, and her lines were still limited in number.

It was the painting, the concept, that had changed. Here was a picture of a tree reaching up, struggling up with top-branch greenery, to the skies, here was a splash of the blue and a single white cloud above it, and here at the side, a rose.

A tree with green leaves reaching for the sky. And at its side, separate but close at hand, this rose in bloom.

Our Garden of Roses.

I remembered the story of the King who had a priceless jewel of which he was very proud. One day quite by accident the face of the stone was scratched. Try as they might, the finest artisans in the kingdom could not erase the scratch from the stone. There came into the kingdom a lapidary artist of surprising genius. He took the stone and on the face of it he carved a rose—of the scratch he made a stem.

This was what we were doing in our school. This was our rare garden of roses.

Chapter 15

‖‖‖

Yet even as our school was putting down roots into reality, as all of these delightful activities with our children evolved and expanded I was engaged in battles on political fronts for our very existence as a school.

We were still—even with faculty, classrooms, students, program and achievements—not a school at all. Technically, we were only rental property, property rented by, run by and officially under the command of the Nassau County Vocational Education and Extension Board.

For months I had been engaged in conferences and discussions, all designed to get what we wanted—a legislative victory in Albany that would give us existence, a legal entity, independent of any board with a legal charter to carry on this work which we believed was in the process of achieving a major educational breakthrough for these disabled children.

At all times in this effort we had the full backing of Governor Rockefeller. His promise to me that harried afternoon of his visit to Abilities was no mere gesture. He knew the need—as Ray Simches and many of us working intimately with disability knew the need—for a fresh approach to the tried techniques of most traditional teaching and training programs for the disabled. Too little had changed in half a century or more.

Something else was needed—a new look, a fresh orientation.

One way in which an independent school and faculty could be achieved—one that could demonstrate new and effective ways of dealing with this problem—would be through a separate school. Governor Rockefeller had recognized this too, he knew the need for good facilities for education of even the less-severely disabled in New York State.

All of that was in my mind way back in the winter of 1963, when I went to Garden City to call on the man Rockefeller had asked to assist in our matter—Assembly Speaker Joseph Carlino.

It was a large, comfortable office. Carlino sat behind a desk. He puffed on a cigar—a well-dressed, handsome, relatively youthful, softspoken man with a quiet kind of firm eloquence.

Two other men were with him, political leaders in school districts where our school and its role might be of some importance. They were cordial when I arrived, accompanied by the Human Resources Foundation counsel, Jack Coffey. Carlino asked us to sit down. There was an air of expectancy. Their silence seemed to ask: "Well, if this school idea of yours is so good, give the reasons why."

So we began to talk, to tell them.

I started by telling them about some of our children, some of the stories of what they had done already—about the little girl who was going to have an operation on her arm until our recreational therapy program in the summer camp made it unnecessary, about the junket into town to the museum, to the television studio, the yacht trip they had taken, the supermarket.

I told them about the boy with stumps who wouldn't go in swimming because he didn't want anyone to look at him without his specially-built boots—until I took off my artificial limbs and went in swimming with him.

I told them other deep-reaching reasons. "Because, you see—this is a new kind of school. Although curriculum content didn't exist for our school, it has to be shaped, forged, no one has ever written a complete curriculum on recreational therapy for such children or one for adaptive physical education. Nobody ever has written the curriculum for an art teacher to follow in teaching a student with a severe deformity from arthrogryposis or arthritis, some child who can't hold a pencil or chalk. They just said—excused from art.

A course in home economics had to be redesigned.

"Nobody ever designed a science curriculum so that the students on the litter or the wheelchair could conduct research experiments. They said, excused from science. Excused from gym. Excused from music. Excused from school. Excused from—life."

I was aware Carlino knew that New York State schools lacked special education teaching facilities to a degree that students with physical disabilities were being sent to other states, at a substantial cost to our taxpayers.

"This school is a pilot then, a demonstration?" one of the local leaders asked.

"It's an opportunity to change the thinking of several million people, families, students themselves, doctors, teachers. To open the eyes of schools everywhere."

"You think you could convince other communities that they should have schools like the one you are building here?"

"Why not? The destiny we want for our children is that—if they can and when they can—they should go to the regular schools, not special schools. Perhaps by what we do regular schools will change to some degree so that many can attend. But while they can't attend regular schools, where do they turn?"

In any such program as we are presenting, it was normal for officials to be somewhat cynical, because so many people are asking really only for a handout. And we show up—somebody else with a big idea to shake the world. And even though the Governor himself supports it, the others want a hard, long look.

But as we spelled it out, the whole atmosphere changed. Suspicions were gone. Carlino and his associates began to consider it. Who would be against such a plan, such a school? After a few brief words on the technical details of handling a piece of legislation, he said to me, "Hank, you go see Phil."

Carlino was chairman of the State Senate's all-powerful

Rules committee beyond which no piece of legislation moved unless the committee approved. Phillip J. Bisceglia of Long Beach, Long Island, was the committee's legislative counsel—Carlino himself called him "the traffic cop" because Bisceglia presides over the movement of hundreds of bills in the state assembly.

Now it became clear what the Governor meant on his visit. What we were after, at that moment, was legislation to establish a school for these homebound, severely disabled children with normal minds, a privately-operated but state-sponsored school of a wholly new kind, a pilot, demonstration program for the state. At the State House in Albany, I found Bisceglia around the corner from Carlino's office working away in a small office crowded with a thousand documents. This is a remarkable man, a bundle of dynamic drive and energy—and a powerful figure on the legislative floor. One columnist described him as being "forever immersed in a blizzard of paper."

As seen by this political columnist, Stan Hinden, Bisceglia "is rarely interviewed. It is not that he shuns publicity. He is just hard to catch. One of the most familiar sights in the capitol is Bisceglia's small, round figure hurtling into the Assembly chamber, up to the rostrum, down to the floor, into the speaker's office, down the hall, into the Ways and Means office and then out of sight, soon to reappear from a different direction. A dozen times a day, Carlino snaps: 'Get Phil,' and the words 'Find Phil' echo through a long chain of secretaries . . ."

Bisceglia and I talked in his office. Carlino had filled him in. The story, I could see, was something that touched him deeply. Also, Long Beach, his home town, was not far from us. "I am coming into your place to see you. I want to see all the plan," he told me. "I'm taking a flying trip down there."

So this busy, friendly, Albany-based political expert, with a thousand other things to worry about at once— items that had far more political significance—took the time out to come to see our people, our children, our school.

Maybe there was other legislation that mattered more. In comparison to other problems ours was not the most important thing on the whole docket of bills. But Rockefeller, Carlino and Phil Bisceglia gave it their personal attention. For none of them did it have political implications or importance. It was simply something in which they could believe.

Bisceglia took the time out from his duties in the post in Albany on several occasions to confer with me to give me the benefit of legislative draftsmen with whom we conferred on the actual wording of the bill.

The bill finally was written. It was introduced into the legislature and, amid the rush and debate on far more important matters than ours, taxes, and motor vehicle laws and liquor taxation questions, the small item was passed smoothly and without opposition. When it reached the Governor's desk, there were a few other organizations that sounded off and tried to hold up the legislation but it was only a last-minute flurry. The bill was signed into law. Our school was now recognized.

It was a bill relating to "an experimental, demonstration, pilot" project, according to the title, "The People of New State of New York, represented in Senate and Assembly, do exact as follows:

"Whereas the State of New York is committed to the development of educational programs for all its pupils and the promotion and development of programs for physically handicapped children in public shcool classes so that they may benefit from the many advantages inherent in group instruction, notwithstanding the provisions of any general or special law to the contrary, the commissioner of education may, in accordance with an equitable method adopted by him and approved by the director of the budget, appropriate and pay to the Human Resources School, such sums of money as may be authorized by the legislature for the instruction of severely handicapped children who prior to admission in such school have been receiving home-instruction, attending out-of-state schools or have been exempted from school because their disability or combination of disabilities is such to make them ineligible for or unable to receive instruction in regular schools. The Human Resources School shall be subject to the visitation of the commissioner and submit to the commissioner such reports as the commissioner may from time to time require . . ."

The official to whom we reported directly, however, was the head of the Bureau of Handicapped Children in Albany—our friend Ray Simches, who had done so much to help us from the start.

All the time this battle was in progress, I had been working on actual plans of the building we needed. The grant from the Educational Facilities Laboratories had enabled us to get a wealth of research on the architectural problems.

The plans which emerged were shaped by the thinking of many experts, the architectural department at the Rensselaer Polytechnic Institute, with the aid of a special group of picked students at their architectural school, by our consultants, our own teachers and students in actual classroom discoveries of needs and problems. Details of the designs and concepts were changed frequently.

The emerging blueprint became quite definite. The designs called for delightful recreational areas, a covered walk around the school, so that the children can leave buses without getting wet in rain. The building itself divided into three basic components—pre-school and primary, junior high, and senior high, each divided into four classrooms. The pre-school and primary have their own playground outside the building with sandboxes and garden areas. There will also be a greenhouse, specially designed to handle disabled children, wide enough to accommodate wheelchairs, with specially constructed potting areas where the children can conduct experiments with growing plants.

In the administration area there will be, in addition to regular staff offices, a conference room where visiting educators and student teachers can observe the student classrooms over closed-circuit television, as the school has as one of its main objectives teaching others, demonstrating these new techniques by which disabled children can be taught. The children are aware that this is part of the program and are fully adjusted to the idea; both students and teachers agree that closed-circuit television is a better method than interrupting classes to permit visitors to drop in.

With this is a plan to set up television taping procedures so that the school can "bring in" to the classrooms places where it is difficult for our children to go—some event in New York or in some other city. The school staff would supervise this kind of television taping as a regular educational procedure. The tapes could also be used by other educational institutions, particularly those concerned with the disabled.

Planned also is a special arts and crafts room that will attempt, as Dr. Russ Housman puts it, to eliminate the "basket-weaving" theory of art for the disabled. It will be adjacent to an art and sculpture court for outdoor art work in good weather.

Here there will be exhibits—each month a new "picture of the month" will be shown and there will be also specially built machines for studying colored slides of great paintings and sculpture. If the children cannot go to all the museums of the world, their works of art can be brought vividly and with minimum loss of color or excitement to the children through the miracle of these modern photographic slides.

There will be a unique science laboratory where again

audio-visual aids such as slides can be utilized, where physics and chemistry problems can be explored at facilities designed to enable the students to experiment without danger and without getting out of their wheelchairs. There will be a soundproofed music room for listening, teaching, practicing. There will be a specially designed and adapted medical department.

In addition to the regular classrooms small classrooms will permit teachers to work with individual students or with small groups involved in projects requiring individual instructions. As part of vocational training there is to be a computer pavilion, where young people can work with and learn the latest techniques and skills in computer science and data processing.

The blueprints include an outdoor playground and camping area, science pond, where algae are grown, and other scientific experiments are made. There is to be a softball field, basketball facilities, a picnic area, a nature walk area, a nine-hole miniature golf course to be played in wheelchairs, and outdoor learning pavilions, shaded areas where in good weather teachers may conduct classes out of doors.

One of the most important rooms, perhaps the most important, is the laboratory for everyday living. This is an extension of the home economics courses to meet the problems of everyday living for our children. Here are two separate kitchens—one fully adapted, the other partially adapted. The fully adapted kitchen has all the special equipment the disabled might need—electric stoves low enough to be used easily from a wheelchair, mixing bowls sunk into wooden boards so that they will remain firm if a one-armed individual is mixing salad or omelet *aux fines herbes* or some similar delicacy. There is a receding wall area where packages may be placed. This kitchen also includes electric can openers that can be used with one hand. All cabinets are arranged for easy reach from wheelchairs.

The second kitchen is not so fully adapted for the disabled but serves to teach the youngsters who may not be in a position to afford the best in latest gadgets. It provides equipment for training in how to use a gasflame stove safely, how to light an oven safely, how to put food in the broiler, how to pour out hot water; it is a training area in a hundred safety items that might, especially for the disabled persons, make the difference between life and death.

Part of the Laboratory for Everyday Living is a sewing area where the children learn to make and design clothes to meet their own needs. Also another section is given over to shower stalls, bathtubs and toilets. Training is both in using and caring for this equipment—how do you get into a bathtub; how do you slip from the wheelchair onto a small bench and from that bench slide onto the next one, under the shower?

An all-purpose auditorium is planned, complete with stage and ramps, where assemblies and similar meetings can be held, and theatrical performances staged. It is planned that all equipment will be so arranged that the children themselves, despite disabilities, will be able to

stage the entire production—under the direcion of teachers—but entirely on their own. This will be an all-purpose
room suitable for recreation and group games.

And at the heart of the school—the library. This will be
housed in a special, pleasant room, complete with easy
chairs, lounging nooks and an open woodburning fireplace.
It will open onto the interior greenhouse.

With the charter approved by late spring of 1963, and
signed by Governor Rockefeller, I was able to begin a full-
scale program for raising funds for our building. The designs were adaptive to changing needs—but funds were
essential to make this an actuality.

I had to find—in a period of less than a year—approximately $860,000 for this school. In the course of raising
this money, I went to leading foundations, to individuals,
to corporations and presented our story.

The results were encouraging. The importance and
meaning of what we were doing was recognized. There was
warm response. From foundations, from individuals, close
associates of Abilities, Inc., from people who heard of our
work and voluntarily sent in pennies and dollar bills, we
raised in the course of the next nine months, on a private
appeal basis, enough to begin construction.

The rest we pray will come.

We would start in early spring, 1964. In the late fall and
early winter of 1963-64, I began to make actual plans for
beginning construction. I learned that some of the property
we had originally purchased for Abilities, while zoned for

business use, was not zoned for construction of a school; it would require a variance from our village zoning board.

Routinely we made our application for this variance in the zoning laws. However, it proved to be far more than a routine matter. A group of neighbors in new homes nearby objected. They did not want a school for disabled children to be located so close to their homes.

They had many reasons we were informed. They were concerned about traffic problems, about increased activity along the highway. They also objected to a fence we had put up; instead of a stockade fence it was an open mesh fence and they could see through it.

We had come this far on a long road. We had a charter from the state to run a school on our own. We had plans, designs, blueprints; we had almost three-quarters of a million dollars raised, in the bank or pledged. We had a faculty, we had students, we had a carefully evolved and evolving curriculum. The state legislature had passed a law designating our school as a special pilot project. The building would be constructed at no cost to the taxpayers.

We had come this close.

Now the neighbors said no. They didn't want our school building that close to them, our school building—our children on crutches and in wheelchairs, wearing braces and artificial limbs and articulated hands.

They had their reasons, about the traffic, the noise, many reasons that sounded good to them—although how could a handful of children really cause that much traffic, that much havoc?

The struggle lay ahead for all of us, them and us, for we were not ready to surrender without a fight.

A hint of the underlying feeling of some of these neighbors was expressed more openly at a meeting that was to come a little later in the battle, at a zoning board hearing when one of the protesting neighbors, not realizing whom she was addressing, said to the mother of one of our children, "Let's be frank about this. If you had to look out of your kitchen window at a child in a wheelchair, don't you think that would be a horrible sight?"

And the woman to whom she spoke turned around and said, "I have a child in a wheelchair and I think she is very beautiful."

I could not tell where it would go, where it would end. Suddenly, all the past and all the words of the past crowded into my mind—children on the street crying out, "Ape Man, Ape Man!"

The battle was joined—this ultimate struggle with the neighbors, this symbolic, bruising hour of truth for these neighbors, these children and this school.

Without the permit all was lost. How could we build? What would we do with our children?

Part IV

Battleground

Chapter 16

For me, this sudden open warfare with some of my neighbors represented more than challenge; it was failure—failure of ideas for which I had fought many years here where Abilities had grown to be world famous, setting the pattern for similar plants in thirty-two countries abroad, here at the very heart of my pilot demonstration to prove that the disabled should not be read out of the human race.

Now it came to me on my own doorstep. Certainly they had their sound reasons, from their own point of view, and, as I explained in a brief talk to the children themselves, after they had begun to hear the neighbors' opposition to the school, "This is a democracy where each of us alone or collectively has a right to his point of view, to object to whatever he feels is harmful to his best interests, and we have to respect their right to do this—even when we think they are wrong . . ."

I told them this, but in all honesty I was greatly disturbed and I am sure they knew it. This was the showcase of the disabled—and here you could see our people, our children, our school, in classes, at work, in the plant, here we tried to build good will in a thousand ways, in a beautiful building that could fit into any community. Leaders of American life, Dr. Rusk and Mrs. Roosevelt, Governor Rockefeller, President Kennedy, Bernard Baruch, Sargent Shriver and many other notables—hundreds of them had come here and gone away with praises for what we were achieving.

But these others were saying no—for this or that reason —we do not want these children and this school here.

The arguments were on various grounds. First it was the fences. Then it was the buses that turned around in the driveway, coming and going to school twice a day five days a week, with an occasional trip to the airport or supermarket or whatever it was! Then it was the trees: we were cutting down too many trees—they happened to be *our* trees, on our own property. We would hear reports of these things; sometimes we would get phone calls from one of these neighbors who was opposed to us, explaining why they were upset. It almost seemed as if when one thing was settled, another problem cropped up.

Then came the announcement: The Zoning Board hearing was to be held on April 1, 1964. Unofficial reports were heard that a group of the neighbors would be on hand to present their objections. Petitions were being circulated. They were hiring a local lawyer, it was said.

They were prepared to wage a legal battle to keep us from building this school here in Albertson—from carrying out this extraordinarily beautiful plan with its gardens and greenhouses and nature walks.

It was all wrong, they said. It shouldn't be.

Anyway, not so close to them.

There was something familiar about it, something that struck deep to the hearts of every single person in Abilities, anyone who had carried around with him a serious disability from which, too often, people turned. How many times had we heard the reasons for not being hired, not being wanted!

Of course they loved our children, they loved all crippled children, as much as anybody in the world. Surely we knew that, we understood that. But they had other substantial reasons for not wanting the school so close to home.

Perhaps they could not realize, not being one of us, how many times these children are not wanted by the onrushing world, in different ways, for different reasons.

Most of these neighbors were young married people. The homes were newly built and relatively expensive; most of the couples had children of their own. They were people of some means, the husbands were young businessmen in many instances, people who had moved recently from other areas, including crowded city areas, into these new homes. They knew when they bought these homes that we owned adjacent land. We had been there for some time.

It was understandable that they would want to protect their property and their community in their new homes from any area that seemed to them to be possibly harmful.

We simply did not agree that our school could be harmful or that our children presented a problem. They would be in classes most of the time. They could hardly be too raucous at their play. Indeed, the nature walks would be of value by increasing the beauty of the land.

We had always had a certain measure of environmental opposition. When we began Abilities we had to fight for our rights to build it; at that time we had convinced the Zoning Board that we would not harm the essentially residential character of the community. Through the years we had not done so.

One section of the original property on which we were planning to build the school was zoned for a supermarket. Under this special type of zoning, only thirty per cent could be built on, the rest had to be open, presumably for parking. We wanted a variance to build on thirty-three per cent. The rest of the property we planned to use was listed as residential. We needed no variance here. Already, by the possible protest, our spring ground-breaking schedule for the school was threatened. If it were a protracted legal battle that went into the courts we could be held up for months, even years. We had to win.

I was in Florida with my wife and daughters for a working holiday. There is an Abilities operation in Clearwater. Word came that a group of residents officially were going to object to the variance when the Zoning Board convened to hear our petition.

I decided to fly back.

April first was sunny but chilly. I went over to the hearing room with some of our people in the station wagon. Frank Gentile was along, Dick Switzer, Jack Coffey, our counsel, Bobbi Housman, some of our parents and some of our children.

It was a mixture in the crowded zoning board hearing room on the second floor of the North Hempstead Town Hall. On one side were the protesting neighbors, well-dressed, with their children, their whole and healthy youngsters who probably had very little notion of what this was all about.

On the other side were our people, a handful of parents and disabled youngsters in wheelchairs, and a few adults. There were also other persons from cases to be heard and a number of curiosity seekers who had learned about the protests against our projected school as well as supporters on both sides. It was a crowded room.

Their two attorneys went before the Zoning Board as the first case was called. Before any actual argument could be heard, their lawyer made an appeal for a delay explaining that he had come into the case only recently. He needed time to study it more carefully, to prepare his presentation, to call witnesses. He pointed out that all of these people were sincerely fond of children who were disabled, that they all knew of the wonderful work done by Mr. Viscardi; however, there were other technical and legal matters involved that compelled them to oppose the variance. He asked for a postponement until May or June. The Zoning Board felt this was excessive. They set the date as April 22. They firmly declared that they would hear the matter at that time.

But the postponement was granted. Three weeks were lost.

We filed out of the hearing room; the neighbors and their children, our parents, our youngsters and our staff. As Frank Gentile in his chair was being helped down the steps to the street I heard someone say, "Darling, look out for the cripple."

It didn't matter. Nothing mattered. They had won a delay. It meant that we would have to put off breaking ground for the school.

A few days later, I wrote a report to one of my associates regarding these latest developments:

"Before I flew back to Flordia to rejoin Lucile and the little ones, I called Dr. Parker of the Community Church and asked for his prayers. He was incensed to think that this kind of battle could happen in our community and agreed he would do far more than pray for us, he would be at the hearing to testify on our behalf.

"I then called Monsignor Bermingham, Pastor of St. Aidan's Parish nearby, and he, too, assured me that we would have his active support.

"Frank Gentile called one of the local Rabbis and he agreed to turn out the entire synagogue if necessary to be at the hearing to speak for us.

"Apparently some in the community are disturbed by what is happening and have come forth to help us. The issue, of course, still remains in doubt but I think that all of us feel a lot better about the possibilities of success than we did on the morning when we last saw you . . ."

But I had no idea at that moment—grim and disappointing as was this delay—what a bleak experience awaited us at the hearing to come.

Chapter 17

The April 22nd hearing was extremely difficult for me. I had no personal stake; my work, my own career, my own life, home, family, success—all this I had.

I was fighting only for the school. And here, by my own community, my own neighbors, I was in effect put on trial. I had to prove myself. I had to stand for hours and try to prove I was an honorable man who could be trusted in his own community.

I had not expected this. It was an ordeal I had not looked for.

I had to listen to a group of noisy, shouting, angry people who many times interrupted the proceedings and the witnesses with cries of, "Who are you? We didn't hear your name." In the corridors of the Town Hall during recesses, there were angry interchanges of words.

It was a sickening spectacle.

In the weeks between the two hearings, we had prepared our case carefully, had gone over the situation carefully with the School's Board of Trustees, with many who had stood with us; all had agreed it was not wise to become emotional, to indulge in any wild oratory. I would keep what I had to say a calm appraisal of the facts. The facts would do the talking. Our board felt that I should not fight back too rigorously—but present the facts with quiet dignity.

Many people had come forward on our behalf, several agreed to appear and were on hand. During those weeks we also had had many phone calls from supporters of the cause of the protesting neighbors. Some of the staff had had half a dozen calls a day, from people arguing and debating the issues, stating in effect that we were doing things that were wrong.

I asked Frank Gentile, who received a major portion of these calls, as the administrative head of the school, and he said:

"I told them we're not planning to put any nude freaks out there for the neighbors to stare at. It was going to be a rehabilitation program; everything would be improved, there would be beautiful scenery. It wouldn't be any different to watch our children get out of a bus than watching their own children get out of a car or bus. They're not living in the play yard or gardens. Their schedule isn't going to be eight hours a day in the yard. This is the dream that we have had for years and it's finally coming true. And not only Hank, but the parents and Washington and everybody is in back of this. It's the greatest thing since the Gettysburg Address."

The hearing room itself was crowded—the protesters, their children, friends of both sides, our staff and our volunteers and the parents of our children. There were so many in the room they had to bring in extra chairs.

The attack started almost at once: the attorney for the neighbors asked that our petition be thrown out, because there was a newly issued manual on the zoning laws, out only a few weeks, and our petition referred only to the old zoning manual.

If granted it meant more delay, while we drew up a new petition. The Commissioners recessed to consider this question and returned after some minutes to deny the petition.

During that recess, arguments and discussions were carried on in the hall outside the hearing rooms. Most of this involved the women, those who supported the cause of the neighbors, and our volunteers and the parents of our children. Words exchanged were sharp and bitter.

The lawyer then tried to get the Chairman of the Zoning Board to disqualify himself on the grounds that he was prejudiced. The chairman happened to have a long and distinguished record of service on this board. He denied that he was in any sense prejudiced.

The hearing went on.

Jack Coffey, our attorney, presented the facts and the law. I was the first witness, speaking in favor of the school. I did not talk long, nor emotionally; I gave them a brief outline of Abilities, how we had built our buildings for disabled workers; how little trouble there had been—indeed virtually none at all—in our relationships with our neighbors over these years. I told of constructing the

Human Resources Foundation building, with its medical and research laboratories, its special gymnasium and swimming pool; I told of its purpose as our research arm, for medical research into disability in relation to work programs.

I told them of the need for the school, to show the world how to educate the severely disabled child, to show the world what can be done with these children.

I brought out the magnificent plans for our school, plans on which we had spent so much time and effort, with so many details changed and rechanged to achieve the finest and best school possible. Whatever else happened, we all knew that it was in the kind of school we created, the calibre and achievement of that school, its staff and its students, that would hold the final answers.

The attorney for the neighbors rose and asked if he might be permitted to cross-examine me.

The hearing room was jammed; there was standing room only in the back and every chair available in the building had been crowded in. I stood as I gave my statement to the Board. I also stood throughout the lengthy cross-examination. How could I doubt our victory? Clearly, we had a right to build the school. The opposition tactics were primarily delay and postponement.

The opposing attorney began by attacking me and Abilities on several different grounds. The landscaping that we had done, as we had promised, had not been enough, had not been sufficient. Hadn't we promised never to build any more buildings—and hadn't Mr. Viscardi reneged on many of these promises he had made earlier? Could I be trusted to keep promises now?

Did we pay land taxes? No, we were tax exempt; this was rehabilitation through work therapy. That was the whole purpose of Abilities, a demonstration center. This had been decided years ago by the Federal government. Did we actually produce and sell products? Yes, we do. How many trucks come in and out of Abilities every day? I tried to answer this on an average, but for the life of me—what did that part have to do with the school, where no trucks at all were involved? Abilities has been running for years and was not at issue in this matter. It had long provided a needed service to the community and had gotten along well with its neighbors. It had no issue before the Board.

The questions kept on. Weren't we really a factory? I said no, we were not; but the questions still kept on this line: was it right to have a school this close to a factory? Wouldn't that be harmful to the children? Never once did he present the real issue. Abilities has long since been accepted. This was a well planned school. The real issue was prejudice and ignorance.

The attorney was quite forceful in his interrogation. At times I felt like a defendant on trial for some capital offense. On one occasion I found it necessary to ask, "Am I on trial here?"

At another point he challenged a statement of mine that we had received a ten thousand dollar grant from the Ford Foundation to research the design and shape of our proposed school building. He produced a letter from an official of the Ford Foundation stating that they had granted no such item to us, so far as their records showed.

This should have been a high point in his case; it was a direct challenge to me, to the reliability of a statement I had made.

I explained to him then that with just a little investigation or questioning he would have learned that the Educational Facilities Laboratories is the education arm of the Ford Foundation and in fact had its offices on the floor directly below that of the main Ford Foundation offices in New York.

I explained that the grant had come from this arm of the Ford Foundation; why had he not bothered to check with them?

I certainly cannot blame any attorney for trying to present the strongest case possible. I was only sorry that in this instance I had to take the brunt of an attack I did not deserve. I was not a defendant; I was not here to apologize for trying to aid disabled children.

It is difficult for me to condone the political expediency of the Zoning Board which allowed this ad hominem attack to continue for hours when it was unrelated to the issue. Nor can I understand the attitude of such an attorney or his clients.

Even during my testimony there were moments of noise, interruptions. When I explained that it was not a factory we had at Abilities but a work center for disabled, someone jumped up and cried out, "I don't care what you say, it's a factory. Brick is brick."

One of our parents managed to get up at that and say, "What about the Herricks School they're building across the road? What are they going to use that for—because I understand that's built of brick, too."

The cross-examination went on. I stood for the entire time. The Board permitted the questions, and made no effort to halt the character of the ordeal under which I was put, I felt, entirely unnecessarily.

A few other witnesses spoke on our behalf. Fred Shore —Dr. Frederick Shore of the East Meadow school district on Long Island and Dr. Ben Wallace of the Mineola school district. They spoke of how good it was to have a place like this where youngsters in need of our kind of school could go, how much it meant for severely disabled children in their districts to be attending such a school.

Rabbi Roxkoff of the Temple Beth Sholom in Mineola spoke for us. His words were on the moral and ethical issues; the fact that they were God's children, that they should not be shunted away into some sylvan glen where no one would see them or be with them, that this school was bringing them into the light of God's world, into His sunlight and His care—not hiding them away.

Reverend Couch, pastor of the Manhasset Congregational Church, spoke of what this facility was doing, of the volunteer women from his own church who were serving on our staff, working with our children, the spiritual meaning of this work to the children, to the volunteers themselves, to the community.

Among the witnesses for the protesters were three ladies

who presented the neighbors' attitudes effectively, and clearly. Their general approach was that they were in favor of everything I was doing, they admired and respected my work and my objectives; they certainly were not fighting against the idea of a school for such children; but it should be on some beautiful estate, somewhere in the quiet of woodlands away from any central community —some beautiful building—somewhere else.

One of the Commissioners asked if it wasn't always this way—we like what you want to do, but not here. Does anybody ever want this kind of building near him?

One of the women, a former homebound teacher herself, had her arms outstretched to show how much she felt for the work I was doing and its importance to the world. She believed in this work, and in our school. But somewhere else.

In the corridors after this part of the lengthy hearing, during another recess, there were again explosive arguments. Some of the supporters of the other side began to challenge Fred Shore—if he felt so strongly about it, why didn't they take the children in his school? Some of the opposition raised the question that the school might lower property values in this new development. When one of the homeowners said this might be true, Fred Shore offered to buy his house on the spot at the original selling price. The homeowner did not take him up on the offer.

Despite the emotionalism kindled at the hearing, I felt we had presented our case strongly and well; we had stood up to all the challenges. We had good answers and we had presented them to the best of our ability; we had not tried to run away from them or evade the questions.

I was not prepared for the denouement when the attorney for the opposition asked for another adjournment. He felt that he had to bring in expert witnesses to show how the traffic pattern would be affected in the neighborhood with our school, and psychiatrists and educational experts to show how the school would be indeed harmful to the children, because they would be close to a factory and because they would be in an environment where people did not want them.

He asked for an adjournment to bring in these experts.

Our children were waiting back in the school, as interested as we were in the outcome, waiting for us to bring back a report of victory.

But we had no victory.

The Board agreed to give him three more weeks, a postponement to May 13th—to round up his expert witnesses to prove that building our school would be detrimental to the health and welfare of the community.

Three more weeks' delay! Six weeks in all and he was still not prepared. And the Board did not yet have courage enough to make a decision.

He was going to get expert witnesses—experts to tell us about disability!

I had bitter thoughts on leaving the hearing.

It was twenty-five years since I received my first set of artificial limbs in New York City. Much of my life since then, the greater part of those years, I had devoted to the cause of the disabled. I was no superman but I had given whatever strength I had to working with and for disabled people.

Soon after I received those artificial limbs, war had started and I became a field officer in the American Red Cross. Working with the men in the Army was a new experience, not only in the camp maneuvers but in human suffering, separations, misunderstandings, the devastation, the dead—who could describe it all?

Then when the war was over came a new career working in industry. How well I remembered the limbless, the disabled veterans I had come to know. All of this before I started Abilities, Human Resources, the camp, the school.

Whatever I have learned of the complexities not only the disabled but all people must face in life, I have learned from direct and personal experience. If I am a cripple, I must consider myself an emotional not a physical cripple. For I have been struggling to serve the cause of disabled people everywhere; my reaction to this attack on us was emotional. Leaving the hearing room, I prayed for the most needed grace of an understanding heart. I have faith in people, all people; I did not like this deep resentment that welled up within me at the treatment we had received.

And I wondered what these experts on whom this lawyer would call could tell us, the disabled, about disability and disabled children and their problems.

Chapter 18

I came away from this hearing with a seething sense of outrage. Why should we have been put through this kind of ordeal and questioning? Were we miscreants, criminals, despoilers of the public weal? Did I have to take the brunt of an attack on me personally, on my purposes, my integrity?

Had I failed? Was my life's work to be so questioned here in the community where I began, where I lived? What did world acclaim mean when I had not convinced my neighbors?

I was angry not merely for myself; I was angry for this cause, for this treatment, for this series of delays that had already disrupted our plans and schedules for the Human Resources school building. And who could tell how long, how many months it could drag on?

We had a right at least to an answer. We had a right to a decision. If the Zoning Board found against us, we could take it into the courts. The battle could be long and drawn out. But I felt confident of the ultimate results.

And if that was what it had to be, a battle, a real

knockdown street fight with some of the neighbors—I had already made up my mind. I had prayed for wisdom and discernment but if anyone thought I was afraid, if anyone expected me to fold up under pressure, if they thought I was crippled at heart because I had no legs—they were wrong.

The mood of anger was not mine alone. Throughout the community, the school, the staff, the working force at Abilities, there was a mounting cry for action. We were being pushed around by these delays, these charges, these attacks upon me.

Some of my people came in the morning afterwards, with questions.

"How long is this going on?" one man asked. "Do we just sit here and take it?"

"How about a picket line somewhere in protest? How about it? A picket line—everybody in wheelchairs."

"Or a march down Main Street—in wheelchairs—with placards."

They were half joking, and deadly in earnest. The story of the hearing had left deep marks as it had spread through Abilities. As reports spread about the kids waited to hear what had happened—and heard this story.

Word of this potential wheelchair brigade—over which if once started I might have no control whatsoever—spread quickly. I tried to calm it down; nothing like that was really going to happen. But I did not, could not, hide the fact of my own anger nor my disappointment in myself and in those responsible who had allowed this to occur.

I told one important community leader, when he called to soothe the ruffled waters, "All we're asking is a decision one way or the other. We're ready for an all out fight, as long as it takes, as much as it takes, and we'll win, I assure you of that. We'll win."

"Look, Hank, we're your friends. Everybody's with you. We're for you and your people."

"Great," I said. "Then let them all prove it by cutting out this nonsense, by standing up for this school. Let's have the decision, whichever way it goes; let them make up their minds. We're tired of being on the hook. If they want a real fight—let's go! Only no more delays. No more postponements."

But the first thing the attorney for the opposition requested on the morning of May 13th, when the third hearing began, was another application for postponement.

The Board asked how long a postponement this time. The answer: Until sometime after June 15th. Unfortunately, he had been unable to get any expert witnesses to come to this hearing. A number of authorities who had agreed to come for various reasons had been unable to make it on this particular date.

The lawyer then said he did have considerable information from these men, in their statements to him and in their writings and references they gave to him, expert opinion that this kind of school would be harmful to the community. And by community he did not mean merely the neighborhood he represented. He meant all of Nassau County.

The Board chairman asked if we would accept this kind

of presentation, even though no one of the authorities cited were present in person for cross-examination. We knew it was empty and meaningless. We had no objection. The hearing went on.

The main burden of their argument against us that morning was that authorities in the field did not believe in segregation of the disabled; they believed that the disabled should be in regular schools, with normal children, leading, as far as possible, normal lives in a normal world to which they could adjust. Who could deny this? If our crippled children could attend regular schools we would want them there.

He cited one school in which there were three crippled children, all doing well; he pointed out that special bathroom facilities had been installed, special bars which they could hold onto with their free hand.

A Board member interrupted at this point to ask, "Yes. But what about a child who has no arms?"

The lawyer said quickly, "Oh, we're not talking about cases such as we saw in the war."

We were not, of course, talking about war cases. But we were talking about severely disabled children who might well have no arms or legs.

Everything this attorney said about the disabled in relationship to segregation was true. All of our efforts are based on the idea that the disabled do not have to be segregated. Abilities itself was designed to show not what we could do as a company but what our people could do as individuals in that company.

When one of our children become so much improved

through our physical therapy that she was considered capable of returning to regular school, from which—just two years earlier—she had been barred by reason of physical disability, we were faced with the true question of our purpose: should we keep her in our special school or insist that she go to regular school?

She herself was deeply attached to us—as we were to her. "It's the first time I've felt really alive," she told me. "All my friends are here."

"But you won't have to give up your friends, you'll see them often. And meantime you'll be meeting life in a different way, back with the world, where you belong now. . . ."

She understood. Going back was a victory, a moving ahead. The girl who was going back into regular school was a far different individual, far more mature and aware than the frustrated, withdrawn homebound child Bobbi Housman had first interviewed for our first summer camp.

This was the key word overlooked by counsel for the opposition in their presentation: *Homebound*.

Ours were not merely crippled children, they were severely disabled children unable to attend schools, children who had problems far beyond a minor disability.

The children we were talking about were segregated by the very process of rejection, by the fact that schools could not take them. They were segregated by the fact that they could not leave that wheelchair—and the doors had to be wide enough to let a wheelchair in.

They were segregated by the fact that some people didn't want to look at them at all.

Yet this was their counsel's argument: that the disabled should be integrated with normal children into regular schools. We did not debate this point. They simply weren't talking about our kind of children.

For our own authorities, we presented our medical director, Dr. Greenspan, and our school psychologist, Dr. Neuhaus. Dr. Greenspan's qualifications as an expert in this field were extensive. In addition to being medical director of our school and Director of Clinical Services, Children's Division, Institute of Physical Medicine and Rehabilitation, New York University, he was an assistant professor at the university, served on the staffs of three hospitals as associate pediatrician, served on two medical boards and was a member of more than ten national and international medical societies and associations.

I list his credits because it seems to me important to show exactly who was speaking for us as an expert on this subject. Dr. Greenspan was a man who knew this field intimately and personally over many years of taking care of children, particularly those with serious disabilities.

The school, he pointed out, had between twenty-five and thirty children of various ages, all of whom had been homebound for periods of from one year to fourteen years. All were on homebound instruction at the time they were taken into the Human Resources School.

He described in medical detail the various types of severe disorders and disabilities, the fact that many severely disabled children, children with diseases that might be progressive but nevertheless left them with years of life ahead

—many of these children are not given any opportunity for social contact, education, rehabilitation. He pointed out that some of our children are unable to feed themselves, to toilet themselves.

He pointed out that we were talking about the children who had these difficulties that could not be handled in most instances in ordinary schools because the facilities, personnel and routines could not serve the disabled child's individual needs.

When asked if it was not true that the disabled can usually learn to manage as well as the normal, his answer was: It depended entirely on the individual disability. A severely disabled boy with one leg and one arm might still climb a flight of stairs. But a boy who cannot leave his wheelchair would never climb those stairs.

As they talked, I found myself thinking of a statue that we had acquired—a statue of a girl on a crutch. I saw it first when I went to the Federation of Jewish Philanthropies. It was in the lobby, a carving in marble of an angelic child, a disabled girl. I learned that it was done by Dr. Maurice Hexter, of the Federation.

It will sit in the garden entrance of our school, this unusual statue, where it will have a setting to match its strange beauty.

I was thinking about this statue during some of that discussion. This was a work of art—a thing of beauty— the statue of a crippled child.

I found myself wondering how many in that hearing room, or anywhere else on earth, really would have under-

stood the full meaning of that statue of a girl on a crutch
—that beauty is in the eyes of the one who sees, if he has
the eyes to see what is there?

Our second witness of that day, Dr. Neuhaus, dealt with
psychological meanings.

Dr. Neuhaus qualified as a clinical psychologist since
1950, had served with the public schools on Long Island
as a child psychologist and had wide experience also with
mentally retarded and emotionally disturbed children, as
well as the physically disabled.

He stressed the psychological benefits of bringing the
severely disabled child out of a life not of mere segregation
but what is too often closed-door isolation. He described
the children he saw when they come to the Human Resources School. "These are children," he stated, "who because they are homebound face the world with a feeling
that it is a frightening place."

He described their attitude when they first saw him:
withdrawn, silent, monosyllabic. In the months at the
school, this whole attitude vanished. Now they face the
fact that they are part of the world, now they greet him
with, "Hi, Doc!"

He said in effect that they thrived on the love and care
they found in a school like ours, and that this was more
important than anything else—love and concern. It was
far more important to have this in a school for such children than to worry about whether people outside the
school wanted them around or not.

And it would be unrealistic, he said, to take these children out of such a school and try to fit them into the standardized routines of a school system of some five thousand normal children.

What he pinpointed was the whole core of the issue, who our children really were. We were not talking about children who could go somewhere else. Somewhere else didn't want them, had no facilities to handle them. Our children had nowhere else to go.

Members of the Board listened with great earnestness to the arguments of both sides. They announced that they would take the matter under advisement.

Decision was reserved. At least, this was better than another postponement.

Once again the strange contingents of the abled and the disabled trouped out of the hearing room and we helped to carry Frank Gentile in his wheelchair and one or two of the children down the stairs and out into the bright spring sun.

Chapter 19

Somewhere near the south shore waterfront, in what formerly was one of Long Island's wealthier communities, there is a home for children. Or once it was such a home. We had a report of a child there, a paraplegic boy whom one of the school districts had heard about. No one had seen the child. The school people thought we might be interested. Bobbi Housman went over to investigate.

The house itself was a rather large one in need of repair. The area is a run-down residential district. This soundless one-time home for children sits in the midst of this faded world.

The first time Bobbi went there, she could not get in; the woman inside told her to go away, she was letting no one in, they were not going to do anything to this child.

Bobbi went back again. The second time she told the woman through the door, "I'm a nurse but I'm not with the Department of Health and I'm not with any social agency. I'm interested in a school and I think you'd be interested in it, too. For Carmine."

"You're not a nurse," the woman said, still not opening

the door. But after a little, the woman said, "All right—if you're sure you are not from any agency trying to—to harm Carmine."

The door opened on a setting out of a Hawthorne novel. The woman standing there was deformed by arthritis, a small, grey, kindly-appearing woman who looked nervously at Bobbi.

"Come in, come in," the woman said.

The furnishings were out of the mid-Victorian era. The woman explained, "You see, once this was a home for children . . . come in here, I'll show you."

She took Bobbi into a large room in the back, where cribs had been set up in rows. But there were no children or infants. "Once they had as many as fifty children at a time," the woman said. "That was long ago."

From information the school people had provided, Bobbi pieced together some of the story. Evidently, this was once a home for children no one wanted, including seriously crippled children. How long this big house had been operated and by whom—how long it had been in disuse—no one appeared to be sure.

"But that was way back, long ago. Now I live here . . . I have only one . . ."

Then Bobbi saw the child, the little boy, in the shadows beyond the big room; a child with a strange beauty in spite of malformations; he had deformities of hands and feet, and his lips twisted on the left side in a paralytic little smile. He was sitting on the ground—this was his permanent position, sitting cross-legged in a Buddha-like position. He could not unbend his legs. He was smiling at Bobbi, a little-boy smile out of those shadows.

"Who is this?" Bobbi asked. "Who is this child?"

"That's Carmine. I've been his guardian since he was a few weeks old . . ."

Bobbi continued her probing, gently, not to alarm the woman.

The woman had records to show that the child had been hospitalized a number of times. It was clear that she loved the boy deeply with a true mother's love and was desperately afraid that someone would take him from her. Despite the woman's fears, Bobbi talked about the school, won the woman enough to get her to agree to bring the boy to Abilities where Dr. Greenspan examined him.

Like Bobbi, Dr. Greenspan found Carmine a fine boy, despite the part-polio deformations. He suggested to the woman—as he has to other parents and guardians how much the school could do for the child in the school. But before that he wanted other opinions in regard to the child's future care, particularly urologically.

The little boy said, "Well, I hope you'll find a way to help me walk, doctor."

That was the way they left it, as the woman and the child went out together, to return to their home.

Dr. Greenspan insisted that the time for action was now. "He needs immediate positive action in the area where we can help. He has to be with children. He has to get out in the world and see that there are things like other types of cars than ambulances that have driven him from institution to institution. The woman obviously loves him and mothers him. But the child needs so much, in so many ways . . ."

So we began making our plans to take this child into our next fall's junior high. Whether it would work out or not, whether this woman whom the little boy called mother would let him come into our school—there were many "if's" in this story. And all the answers lay ahead.

One more child. One more place where we can help—if we can get this child into our school.

The school had to go on and all our efforts, even while we continued to wait for the Zoning Board's action. There was too much to do. Activities could not be curtailed in any event; we would find another route through even if we were turned down. Even without the program for the new building, even if we had to move out entirely, to find another community, some community that would accept us, we would and could operate under our charter as a school.

The whole process went on—interviews with prospective new parents and students. We could be taking twice as many as before, almost fifty children—with a waiting list.

Parents come to see me. Parents of students with us from the start. Parents seeking to have their boy or girl admitted to this school they have heard about.

A mother talked about her daughter who has been with us two years now: "When she was trying to go to regular school and was out so much and missed so much, one of the big complaints was that she did not read, her reading comprehension was terrible. And now she has just finished reading *Gone With the Wind,* and you "can't get her head out of a book; she has started another one this morning. I can't think of the name of it. It's another great big book."

Another mother talked about a summer camp celebration when her husband, at his disabled daughter's urging, jumped into the pool. "Joe isn't particularly fond of swimming. He just went down and down, because he jumped in where it's deep, and he told me thought he would never come up but he did finally and he grabbed hold of the ladder and he said he was so glad he could reach it because otherwise, in a pool full of all those crippled children, he was about to scream for help!"

Parents come in with questions, hopes, plans, complaints. Some are concerned about grades—our marking system is not hard or unreasonable and yet it is not soft either. We consider the individual problem but only in a measure. Others talked about colleges. We were even then starting to talk about colleges around the country; we were sending for college catalogues so that our students could look through them and begin to get ideas about colleges, about the physical facilities.

Some of our children will be going to college. We have already set up a working program with Hofstra University. With the help of the Otis Elevator Co. and a grant from the Office of Vocational Rehabilitation we are cooperating with them to develop a new kind of inexpensive elevator that attaches to the outside of a building—big enough to carry a student in a wheelchair. The future is already start-ing, the glimmering ways of change.

Uncertainty notwithstanding, the plan went on. To meet the evolving changes, to meet the future, our courses had to be the best in education at any given level. In eighth-grade arithmetic we teach such things as expansion of geometric concepts and algebraic language. Our course de-signed for ninth-grade science included chemistry, fire and fire control, energy, forms and transformation, nuclear power, simple and complex machines, aerodynamics and Archimede's Principle, magnetism and electricity, light and sound.

Quite a program for children who once were told they could not go to school at all.

I told one parent who dropped in to see me, the mother of a delightful child, "If I could put my hand upon her and make her whole, I'd want to do nothing more. But we can give her something in life that she can always look back on and remember, a happy time in school, and the apprecia-tion of life that will come from it."

And I said, "Some people don't think we ought to be here at all, this school. They want to get it out of here, to destroy it; but we'll have the best school anybody ever built. And one day we'll have a wealthy alumni, telling me how to run the place, and complaining about our atheltic program."

Chapter 20

By the first of June we had word. The Board had considered the evidence with the greatest of care. The variances we had petitioned for were granted. There was no longer any obstacle before us.

We had our first graduation exercise, for elementary and junior high. It was remarkably like many other similar events in other schools. Perhaps that was the most extraordinary part of its meaning, the very sameness of it, the flowing pattern of school and commencement and graduation.

The Board of Abilities, Human Resources and the school were there—staff, parents, relatives, friends and students, dressed in their very best, girls in white dresses, boys wearing flowers in their buttonholes.

The French elementary classes put on a puppet show—two French playlets, one about a lost dog and another about a boy who wouldn't wear his sweater. The students themselves spoke all the puppet lines—in French. And they sang *Frère Jacques*.

Then the names of all the graduating students were called out, and one by one they came up the ramp to the platform to receive their diplomas.

Afterwards there were the few words by distinguished guests. "And when you are graduated from high school, I'll say to you, welcome to trouble and danger . . ."

I said a few words of my own also about these children and what they meant to me, to see them here. I told them that there were no permanent solutions to human problems, and we must live by faith in God and in people, all people, and in ourselves.

And I talked briefly about their school, and its role in the future, and the fact that within the next months we would break ground for the new building.

The last speaker was the young girl who is going to leave our school, because she was now able to attend regular school. She was very good. She told of what the school had done for her, for all the class, of what it would mean to them in the future, for all their lives. She was sorry to be leaving, and yet she was also so glad, so pleased and proud and grateful.

It was a very touching valedictory speech, delivered very simply and very well. Many of the mothers and fathers and guests—and one or two of the girl students—had tears in their eyes. So did the staff—including me.

There could hardly have been a more normal graduation, anywhere in the world.

And what of future graduations? As our school grows it will become a hope for crippled children everywhere, an example for other communities to follow—a school of tomorrow.

How can we say what this tomorrow will be? Each individual child has his or her own destiny. We can only help. What can we give Rhonda? Perhaps all we can give her is a sense of understanding, that in all the years she lives she can drink in beauty, a play, the sound of music, memories of associations she has had with other youngsters, a sense of purpose and dignity.

These too are priceless gifts.